KING OF THE MOUNTAIN

Also by Pete Fromm:

The Tall Uncut

Indian Creek Chronicles: A Winter in the Bitterroot Wilderness

Monkey Tag

KING OF THE MOUNTAIN

Sporting Stories

Pete Fromm

STACKPOLE
BOOKS

Published by
STACKPOLE BOOKS
5067 Ritter Road
Mechanicsburg, PA   17055

Printed in the United States of America

10 9 8 7 6 5 4 3 2 1

First Edition

Cover painting from an oil by Dale Livezey © 1993 Augusta, MT

A number of the stories in this book have appeared in print previously. "Harper" was originally published in *American Way.* "Megadethed" was originally published in *Game Journal.* "Halibut-head," "Mixed Shot," "Grayfish," "First Time Out," "Trumpeter," "Lost," "Heads," and "Legacy" were originally published in *Gray's Sporting Journal.* "Blues in the Reefs" and "Flyways" were originally published in *Sports Afield.* "Home Before Dark" was originally published in *Fly Rod & Reel,* as the winner of the 1994 John Voelker Fly Fishing Fiction Award.

Library of Congress Cataloging-in-Publication Data

Fromm, Pete, 1958-
       King of the mountain : sporting stories / Pete Fromm. — 1st ed.
              p.   cm.
       ISBN 0-8117-0937-X
       1. Outdoor life—United States—Fiction. 2. Men—United States—Fiction.
3.Sports stories, American. I. Title.
PS3556.R5942K5   1994
813'.54—dc20
                                                                      94-652
                                                                      CIP

To John Pancoast and John Powers,
my partners afield

CONTENTS

Halibut-head

FROM THE BACKSEAT Rick said, "Are you all there, Teddy Ray?" He had to kind of shout over the wind rushing through the windows. "Are you still with us at all? This is a Rambler, Teddy. A Rambler." He started to spell it, "R, A, M . . ."

"Give me the hill," Teddy said, looking determined behind the wheel. The wind tugged at his hair.

"Give me the hill and I can do it. Maybe even a hundred and twenty."

"Piss on one-twenty," I said. "I thought we were going fishing."

"This thing couldn't go one-twenty off a cliff," Rick said.

I didn't say anything. Teddy just kept nodding his head a little, gripping and regripping the wheel. His tongue barely poked out, wetting his fat lips. "A hundred and twenty," he said. "She'll do it."

Without signaling he pulled onto the frontage road. It was rough as a cob, but the cops never bothered anyone there. All through high school it's where we'd done our racing and patch-ing and donuts. I said, "You couldn't hold it on this road over a hundred, Teddy." I was trying to reason with him but he glanced quick at me, like I'd dared him. Soon as I saw that look I fumbled around at my waist, looking for the seat belt. I said, "Come on, Teddy. Let's just go fishing." It was an old Rambler—like there's any other kind—and it didn't have shoulder belts.

Teddy kind of snorted. He was up to seventy-five, going flat out, still on the level. Square Butte was off on our right, the wheat all around us already gone to gold from that heavy green that first makes you think summer'll never end. The big hill dropping to Ulm was just ahead. Rick said, "Hey, Halibut, there's no belt back here. If I can't wear one, you can't wear one." With the wind now he really had to shout.

I glanced back, seeing him already bouncing around a little, the rods and tackle boxes shifting with him as Teddy tried to ease the Rambler around the holes. One of my minnow nets bounced off the deck behind the seat and hit Rick in the neck. He grinned at me.

I looked ahead. The road was all freckled looking and I said, "What's all that?" but then I knew and I said, "Hey, they're grasshoppers." I looked at Teddy Ray. "Let's stop and grab a mess of them for bait."

Teddy didn't say anything, didn't even look at me, and I could hear the hoppers ticking into the grill. One jumped high enough to unfold his wings. He smacked the windshield between me and Teddy and left a long, yellowy green spray on the glass. Rick shouted, "Bet he won't have the guts to do that again!" He was the only one who laughed.

I said, "Come on Teddy, let's round up some bait."

Teddy smiled, just a trace of a smile really. He edged the car over till my side was way on the shoulder. They hadn't mowed the ditches, and the grass came clear to the top of the door. If I'd reached out I could've stuck my hand into it. It would've stung

like thorns though, fast as we were going. The grasshoppers the
car kicked out made a haze above the seed heads. "Stick a net
out the window," Teddy said.

I looked at him and he was smiling pretty big now. We were
on the first slight downhill, leading into the big drop. I glanced
at the speedometer. We were up to eighty, maybe eightytwo.
"Give him a net, Rick," Teddy said. "You stick one out the
other side."

Rick looked at me and shrugged and handed me a net. It
was hard to control; the small mesh catching a lot of air. But
even before I could level it low over the grass I had a couple
hoppers, and I laughed. I said, "Hey, this might work."

Rick said, "I'm too far away. I can't reach anything."

The car lurched to the left, too quick for how fast we were
going, and I pinched my arms against the outside of the car
door, like I could hold myself there once we left the road. But
Teddy brought it back, the driver's side just snipping the grass,
and Rick yelled, "Man, I got a million already!"

Then we were on the real hill, and Teddy didn't let up, like
I'd half expected, or half hoped anyway. The last time I looked
we were doing one hundred and twelve. Then Teddy swung it
my way, and I thought, "This is it for sure, we're into the
wheat." But somehow he saved it, and Rick whooped and
Teddy shouted, "Your turn."

I made a kind of halfhearted attempt to lift my net while still
holding on to the door at the same time. The Rambler was all
over the place, bouncing around like our busted washing
machine at home. Even so my net filled up until it was hard to
hold. It drooped down into the grass and nearly ripped from my
hand. When I pulled it up, the lower curve of the aluminum
hoop was bent backwards. Teddy Ray screamed, "One hundred
and twenty! One-goddamn-twenty!"

I knew he'd keep going until we looked at the speedometer,

so I pretended to and I shouted, "I can't hold the net!" I looked at Rick, to try to make him say the same thing, but we hit the pothole then and Rick shot up into the ceiling and the car started sideways, and I closed my eyes and grabbed the seat, wondering if the stick shift could pierce my skull.

For a long time it seemed the only sound in the world was the screech of rubber skinning off tires, but it finally quieted to where there wasn't even the rush of wind through the windows. I opened my eyes and looked around. First thing I noticed was the shifter up on the column. Three on the tree. Couldn't've gone through my head if it wanted to.

I sat up. We were sideways in the wheat, still pretty close to the road, ditch grass stuck under the windshield wipers. From the floor of the backseat Rick said, "Good job, man. Good job. You almost lost it there."

Teddy Ray was still holding the wheel, still staring through the bug-smeared windshield, still driving, for all I could tell. I noticed a grasshopper crawling up the front of his shirt. There was another one staring at me from the vinyl seat.

I sat up slowly. There were grasshoppers everywhere. On the dash, the seats, the floor, even trying to walk up the windows. I plucked one from my cheek and started laughing. We all started to move then, and Rick said, "Holy shit, I pulled my net in." He held up the net, still half full of big hoppers that hadn't stood the speed of impact. I opened my door and walked through the waist-deep grass to the road. Way back there behind us, back where all the crazy skids started, I could see my net glinting in the sun. "I dropped mine," I said, Rick and Teddy closing in around me.

"You did it, Teddy," Rick said. "Never'd've believed it if I hadn't lived through it. One twenty in Teddy Ray's Rambler. Man, you're a hero." Rick was laughing a little, breathing big, deep breaths of the heavy, sunny air.

Rick and I walked up the hill for the net, but it was trashed, half full of dead hoppers, just like Rick's. I kicked it into the ditch with the beer cans. "You should've pulled it in like I did," Rick said.

"Did you know you pulled it in?"

"Hell, no. Are you kidding?"

We kind of laughed, glad to be able to feel the sun coming off the asphalt and hear the hoppers clatter away from our legs. When we got back to the car, Teddy was just straightening up on the other side. "Blew the tire clean off," he said. "The rim's trashed." He shook his head. "I don't have a spare. You know how much a rim costs?"

Rick said, "You can get one at a junkyard. That's where all the other Ramblers in the world are." I swung the back door open and started handing out rods. "We can walk from here," I said, but Teddy wouldn't leave until we got the car back out onto the road and jacked up, like we'd had a flat. "Cops'd get me for reckless for sure," he said. You could tell he was kind of proud when he said, "Check those skids."

"Rambling Teddy Ray," Rick said, laughing. He asked if Teddy wanted it locked.

Teddy said, "No, leave the windows down. Maybe some of the grasshoppers'll leave."

I took my rod and headed down the road. "Let's go fishing," I said.

"Rambling Teddy Ray," Rick said, a little louder so I could hear, "and the Halibut-head. How'd I ever get stuck with this crew?"

I shouted over my shoulder, "I can't hear you. I'm going fishing." Pretty soon I could hear them running to catch up.

It was hot by the time we got to the river, and Teddy had a blister. He never went anywhere he couldn't drive. He took off his shoes and sat down in the water. Never even strung the line through his rod. Pretty soon he walked back into the grass for a snooze. Rick and I cast all over the place, using everything, but the fishing was no good. There was some tiny bug out, about a trillion of them dead on the top of the river, and I knew any fish that was eating was only eating those. It ruined everything for us. Some guy up the river was doing all right, though, using one of those fly rods, hooking into them now and then, just often enough to keep Rick from quitting right off.

After a while, though, Rick wasn't even carrying his rod. He was just rooting around in the shallows, stirring up mud. I was about to ask what he was doing when the guy upriver tied into a big one, a jumper. The water went all silvery every time it splashed down. I reeled in fast and tied on the smallest spinner I had. It was still about the size of a thousand of those bugs.

I'd made a couple casts when Rick came up to me, grinning so wide I wondered if his cheeks might rip. He held out the biggest crawdad I'd ever seen, its arms out, the claws opening and closing, dying to latch on to something. Rick tossed his head back to where Teddy must've been snoozing.

He was out cold in the grass, a shiny layer of sweat on his face, where his cap didn't cover. He was just overweight enough that it looked like it was his bulk that flattened the grass around him, though either one of us would have flattened it just as easy. He twitched a little as he slept, probably because he was too hot, but Rick whispered, "Look at him, he's still Rambling through that pothole."

Rick waved the crawdad toward Teddy and asked if I thought we could get his fly open without waking him. I said I wasn't going to have anything to do with that. Rick said, "I saw you, Halibut, you were ready to kill him on that hill. Man, you thought you were never going fishing again."

"I don't like going fast," I said.

"Do his fly."

"Just put it on his chest. Scare him."

Rick really was only kidding about the fly, and he set the crawdad on Teddy's chest. It sat there a second, then tried running away, flipping its tail and scooting backwards. I was already backing away when Teddy woke up, brushing at the crawdad before he saw it.

I turned and ran when I saw the curved, blue-gray pincer snap shut at the edge of the nail on Teddy's little finger. When I hit the river, I snatched my rod and headed upstream, looking back in time to see Teddy jumping around, shaking his hand like crazy, the crawdad hanging on for its life. Rick was trying to help when Teddy Ray pulled the crawdad off. Teddy got it turned around so it wouldn't claw him, then started after Rick with it.

They disappeared in the grass pretty quick, but I could hear them swearing at each other, laughing but out of breath from running. They were the only guys I knew, but neither one of them was much for fishing. I'd never wanted to go anywhere by myself before, but for the first time I wished I had a car of my own. I cast a few times and kept wandering upstream, knowing I wasn't going to catch anything.

At the first big bend I bumped into the other guy, the one who'd been catching stuff. He looked up, an old guy, and I could tell he didn't think much of me or my friends. I asked, "How's it going?"

He nodded his head a little and shrugged.

"I saw you hooking into some pretty decent ones." He was holding on to big handfuls of looping line, and more of it trailed in the water. I figured maybe I'd caught him in the middle of a nasty backlash, and I was trying to say something that wouldn't embarrass him. There wasn't any stringer stick I could see, and I thought maybe he'd lost all those fish. With the size of the backlash he had, I figured maybe he was a real rookie. "What're you using?" I asked, figuring maybe that was a better question.

"Trico," he said. "Spent-wing."

"Oh," I said. Maybe he wasn't from around here. Maybe he was a foreigner.

"How about you?" he asked. "What are you using?" He started to smile.

It was reassuring to hear him speak English. I said, "Everything I've got. Nothing works, though. They're eating all these lousy bugs." Then I remembered the big one he'd had on, the way it'd jumped. Even though he'd lost it, I knew he'd had it on. I hadn't had a hit. "You mind showing me one of those Trike things?" I asked.

He opened up this funky, silvery tackle box he had strapped to his chest. He fiddled some, then held out something I couldn't see. I looked at him to see if he was a joker kind of guy, then I slogged through the shallow until I was standing next to him. He held this black hook with white fuzz on it. Whole thing the size of a smallish mosquito. I said, "Uh huh."

Then he plucked one of the dead bugs off his waders and held it next to his hook. They looked the same. "Yeah, but . . ." I said.

"That's what they're hitting," he said.

"Yeah, I can see that." I looked back at the pile of line he had in his hand. He wasn't doing anything to untangle it. "Mind if I watch a second?" I asked.

He shrugged again, and before I was quite ready, he lifted his rod back, quick, then changed direction and brought the rod forward. The whole backlash shot through the eyelets smooth as silk. He lowered his tip at the end of it, and all that snarl of line lay down on the river, straight as a line drive.

He didn't reel in or anything. Just stood and watched his line drift a little, then he slurped it off the surface just by lifting the rod, and he shot it out again and let it drift.

"Why don't you reel in?" I asked. It felt weird talking after watching that smooth, quiet cast.

"Reel just holds the line. The fish takes the fly as it floats."

I said, "Uh huh." I glanced down at my jeans, soaking wet and dark, my sneakers white enough they seemed to glow there on the bottom. Then I looked at him in his fancy chest waders. I wished I wasn't holding my bright yellow Eagle Claw.

"It's too hot now, though. They've stopped feeding. A grasshopper might do the trick for a few of them."

I perked up, wanting to see him cast again. "We got a whole car full of grasshoppers."

He opened his chest tackle box again and picked out something. He held it to me. It was a life-size grasshopper. All the right colors, even had big back kicker legs, bent just right above the wing, coming back down, ready to hop. "Wow," I said. "Where in the world did you find that?"

"I tied it," he said.

I guess I gave him a look then. He laughed right out loud. "Haven't you ever seen anyone fly-fish?"

"I suppose," I said. "Never up close, though." That was true. I'd seen them before at distances, usually in boats. They always looked like such pansies, doing nothing but waving around their long rods while I caught fish. "I never saw anybody cast like you just did."

"Where are you from?" he asked.

"The Falls," I said. Then I laughed a little. "I was wondering the same thing about you."

"Helena," he said. Then he introduced himself, asking what my name was. Before I thought I said, "Halibut." Rick had started calling me that a few years ago, and it kind of stuck.

"Halibut?" he asked, smiling.

"Yeah. Short for Halibut-head. Sort of like Butt-head. But not like that. It was just the dumbest fish name they could think of. It's because I fish too much."

"How could anybody fish too much?"

"Yeah, I know. That's why I don't mind."

"And you've never fly-fished?"

I shook my head.

He looked at me a second, and I felt even worse about that Eagle Claw dangling from my hand. It was so yellow. "Mind if I look at your hat?" he asked.

Now I hadn't expected that. It was a Shakespeare cap that'd come free with a reel. It was in pretty sad shape, and I felt like a bumpkin handing it over. I flattened my hair down. He held my hat just long enough to stick that grasshopper in next to the embroidered patch. I hadn't realized exactly how dirty that hat was till right then. I took it when he handed it back but didn't put it back on. I looked at that hopper, browns and yellows bright against the black hat, looking ready to jump off any second. "Thanks," I said.

"Tomorrow morning I'll be fishing this same stretch," he said. He was reeling in his line. When I didn't say anything he said, "But I'm done for today. Too hot."

I wasn't listening to him real close. I could hear Teddy and Rick splashing just around the corner. Teddy yelled, "Hey, Butt-head, where'd you go?" Rick just shouted, "Halibut," all sing-songy. I wished a giant wave, a tsunami or something, would come along before they turned the corner.

"Sounds like your friends think you've been fishing too much."

"Yeah," I said. "They always do."

The old guy had his line all in, hooking one of them tiny Trikes into a little metal catch near the butt of his rod. "Tell you what, Halibut," he said, smiling at the way the name rolled over his tongue, "I'll bring a spare rod out here tomorrow, if you're interested."

"One like yours?" I said, stalling, trying to think if Mom would be using the car tomorrow, scrambling to find any chance of getting down here without Teddy and Rick and the Rambler.

Then Teddy and Rick broke around the corner that'd hidden them from view. They both had crawdads in their hands, and when they saw me, they crouched low, sticking the grasping claws my way, waving them slow, cooing, "Oh, Halibut? Oh, Halibut-head? Come here a sec, Halibut."

When they saw the old guy behind me, they cut it out a little bit, but they were both dripping wet and red from laughing and they still giggled pretty hard. I turned to the old guy from Helena and said, "I'll be here."

He said, "See you then, first light." He nodded a little at Teddy and Rick and said quietly to me, "Good luck," then went up the short bank, careful and slow, like any old guy. When he was completely out of sight, I threw my Eagle Claw onto the bank. It disappeared in the grass, and real quick I turned and flipped over a big, flat rock I'd picked out as soon as I'd heard those guys splashing around looking for me. It was in a foot of water, right in front of where the old guy'd been standing to cast.

I was pretty lucky sometimes, and this was one. A big, old, grumpy, blue-clawed 'dad was under that rock, froze now in the sudden light, his claws lifted to the sides, waiting. I pinned him down, then lifted him up quick. I turned to where Teddy and Rick were still standing at the corner.

They'd let their crawdads droop to their sides, and Teddy said, "Did you ask that geezer for a ride?"

I said, "No way, toads." Then I arced my left hand behind my head, like a swordsman, and I advanced, holding my fearsome crawdad out front.

"En garde!" I shouted.

Mixed Shot

KEITH GAVE HIS WIFE, Patty, a small kiss to make sure she was asleep, then rolled carefully away from her and edged out of the bed. He closed the bedroom door behind him, turned on the small light in the kitchen, and sat down at the table. He'd laid out his camouflage clothing the night before, and he dressed quickly.

There was frost on the windows. It was late for that, but his clothes would be warm enough. He smiled as the coffee machine made its last splutters and he dabbed on his green and black face paint. Keith filled his thermos, picked his gun case from beside the back door, and walked into the cold night. He closed that door firmly behind him, too.

It was more than a two-hour drive to the turkey grounds he'd scouted all spring. He was on the highway in plenty of time, though, and he listened to faraway talk shows as he drove. By the time he pulled onto the Forest Service road, there was only the faintest hint of light in the east. He turned the radio off. He knew he'd have the timing right. "To a gnat's ass," he said to himself, grinning.

He parked finally, turning off his headlights. The last thing he hadn't had control over was decided. He clenched his fist and said, "Yes!" There were no other cars at his spot, none on the whole road. He'd gone farther than he ever had before, and he'd found the biggest gobbler he had ever seen in his life. Bigger than he would have guessed possible. He'd endured Patty's kidding, and he'd come here every weekend, in the snow at first, until he had found the roosting tree. He had earned this bird, and the only thing he had worried about was whether some joker would blunder into it.

He turned on the cab light of his truck and opened the new box of shotgun shells. They were the kind they had just come out with, the mixed-shot shells, with two different BB sizes in the same shell. The bigger BBs would kill at longer range, and the small ones would fill in the pattern, making the close-in shot lethal. Keith had studied these as thoroughly as everything else. No matter what, they'd kill.

He put ten shells into his vest, filling every elastic loop. He smiled at that, too. A turkey as old as the one he was hunting wouldn't give him a chance for a second shot, let alone a third or a fourth or a tenth. He'd have to do everything right, silently and motionlessly, just to get in range. Then he'd have to be as quick as lightning to get off the one shot he would have. He'd gone over it a hundred times.

He moved into the woods, using a flashlight as far as it was safe. Then he crept on in the blackness, the thick stuff brushing against his thin, green gloves and along his face. He held his shotgun pointed at the ground several paces in front of him. It was loaded, because he was in the turkey area now, and even though it was too dark to shoot, he could not risk the sound the loading would make later.

It was still dark when Keith reached the cover of brush he

had shaped weeks and weeks ago. He slipped into the cubbyhole and pointed his gun in the direction he knew the shot would be.

He checked the lightening of the sky and then did not move again. It would be almost half an hour, he knew, and he settled into it. The frost began to seep into him, but he knew it would not last long, and he could not risk moving now.

With the dawn the sounds of the woods grew. Odd rustlings whispered around Keith, and he smiled at how he still wondered where they came from. He'd been out long enough to know that they just were—that they didn't come from anywhere.

A squirrel chattered, and then Keith heard the turkeys' morning calls. There were a couple quiet hen clucks and then the rip of gobbling. He pictured them in the trees, stretching their legs and necks, ruffling their feathers. He'd always guessed that they'd stretch their wings, but when he had found the roost and spied on it day after day, he found that they launched off the branches with no warning, setting their wings and gliding to the same spot day after day. His gun was pointed at that spot now.

There was another burst of gobbling, and a sudden commotion of stubby wings flapping against squat, heavy bodies. Keith heard the birds breaking through the branches, and he knew something was wrong. His heart beat faster. They never flapped, they just glided, and they did not crash through the branches unless they were startled.

He moved his head very slowly and did not see any turkeys. They'd left the roost too early. It was still nearly dark. Keith moved his head to look in the other direction but still saw nothing. He could hear the turkeys on the ground, behind him, and he couldn't believe how wrong everything had gone. He took his hen call from his pocket and worked the plunger, once, twice, then a third time. Some hens answered, but there was no gobble. Keith knew that the gobbler would want to round up this stray of his harem, and he knew the bird did not always gobble as he moved in to a hen.

Five minutes later it was just light enough to shoot. Keith still wondered what had spooked them early. He doubted a coyote would spook them from their roost. He went over every step he had made between his car and his blind and could not believe he had done anything wrong. The hens had moved away, and he could no longer hear anything behind him. He worked his call again, and before he had hit it a third time, a gobble burst out directly in front of him.

Keith was breathing faster before the gobbling had even finished. He forced himself to bring his gun up so slowly it hurt. He pictured the overwhelming size of the turkey, the white and blue streak of neck and the red flash of head. There was movement in the grayness before the gun barrel, and then a sliver of red shone between the branches. Keith smiled at the cunning with which the old bird had circled around to the lost hen, and he pulled the trigger.

Even as the shot echoed through the dense timber Keith could hear the turkeys behind him take wing, bursting straight up until they cleared the trees and set their wings for the glides. They were breaking branches.

Keith pumped a second shell in, ready to fire if necessary. He did not think he would have to fire a second time, though. He pictured the red and knew he had shot at the head, and that the range was such that the mixed shot would do the most damage.

He waited a full minute to see if the turkey was wounded and would creep from the thicket it had used as cover for its approach to the hen. He smiled again at how crafty the bird had been, and how, even though things had gone unexpectedly, he had done what he had had to do.

As the adrenaline ebbed, Keith realized he did not hear any flopping in the thicket, such as a head shot would produce, and he wondered if he could have missed and if the turkey could have run, not exposing itself to flight. He stood then, and began to edge toward the thicket.

There was not a movement left in the forest, and Keith still saw no trace of the big gobbler. The thicket was even closer than he had guessed, only ten yards from where he had sat, and Keith wondered again if he could have missed. At that range his shot would have been a clump little bigger than his fist. He reached forward and parted the branches with his gloved hand.

Keith's breathing stopped for a moment. In that moment there was nothing in the world except the wiry, little man lying on his back in the thicket, his throat torn away by heavy and light shot both. Though he was as heavily camouflaged as Keith, there was, at the back of his head, the trace of red bandanna, tied around his neck to ward off the morning cold. Keith could see how the man had tried to pull up his collar to cover the red, and Keith saw the scrap of red he had seen through the branches and how it had disappeared with his shot, and he saw that the man made no motion whatsoever, not even a slight rise or fall in his chest. As he turned he saw the wooden gobbler call still in the man's hand. And the last thing Keith saw, before he started to run, was more blood than he had ever seen anywhere.

Keith was running as hard as he had ever run, dead away from the thicket and what lay hidden in it. Later he would think that he had run before he'd even had a chance to see, but now, as the branches whipped and slapped against him, all he could see was the man's throat, and the three small, black spots on his jaw that Keith knew were from the strays of the small BBs of his mixed-shot shell.

Keith was nearly back to his truck before he stopped his panicked flight. He was beginning to think now, and he crept to the edge of the last clearing before the band of conifers that hid the road. Sometimes startled turkeys would end up in this clearing, and Keith knew now that he needed a turkey.

There were three small turkeys in the open, and Keith lifted his gun, and though he was shaking horribly he managed to shoot again. The turkey he shot dropped down flopping, and Keith was running again. He lifted the bird by the throat and carried it with him while he ran. The bird was an alibi, an excuse to his wife for being home early. It beat against his leg, and he could feel the last bit of life settle out of it before he reached his truck.

Keith opened the back of his truck and threw the young, dead turkey onto the tarp he had put in to keep blood away from the carpet. He slammed the back door and got behind the wheel.

He had to get out of the truck again to dig his keys from the deep pocket of his hunting pants. He dropped them once on the floorboards before he got them into the ignition. Keith stopped everything then, and took several deep breaths. He looked back to the woods and wondered what he was doing.

There was nothing he could do for the man, the picture of the torn throat and the motionless chest convinced him of that. Now that he had started to run, what did he have left? If he went back, what could he do? What would he do if the man had a partner, and the partner was already there? The partner would know he had run. Maybe people would think the man might have lived if he hadn't run.

Keith started his truck, still wondering if he should go back as he gently drove forward until he reached the turnaround. He reversed course there, heading back toward the highway, his bowels nearly letting go as he passed his parking spot. He did not see the other trucks until he came to the last cattle guard. There were two of them, both with Billings license plates, like his own. He resisted the temptation to floor his accelerator, and he pulled onto the highway, turning for home.

Keith knew the trail the men from the trucks had taken into the woods. He'd walked it several times himself, before he had discovered his own more direct route. He wondered how many men there were and where the others were. He wondered suddenly if he might have been seen, and he began to drive faster without knowing it.

No one could have seen him. They would have said something. They would have wanted to know if he'd seen anything. They'd want to know where the birds were. They'd want to know everything. Soon everyone would want to know everything. He thought of manhunts and features on *Unsolved Mysteries*, and when he looked down he was going ninety miles an hour and he stepped on the brake.

If he was stopped for speeding right now, the first words out of his mouth would be, "I shot him." He thought about turning around, but when his speedometer read fifty-six, he set the cruise control. Until then he'd forgotten he had one.

Keith's mind went back to the manhunt. No one knew where he hunted. He'd always been secretive about that, and when he found the great turkey he had been doubly so. Even his wife knew only that he went out east every weekend.

He thought of the detective books he'd read and of the television shows he'd seen, and he wondered how he could be caught. His thoughts were a jumble of panic, though, one minute worrying about boot prints and tire tracks, the next wondering how in the world he'd ever get another job when people knew he had killed someone and run. He couldn't sell insurance anymore. A man needed his name to do that.

Keith cursed and cursed and beat his steering wheel. He never should have run. But he couldn't be caught at this. It would ruin him. How could he face anyone after this?

He would have to move. That was it. He could pack up everything and go. But it was the middle of the school year. His wife had a job. How could he explain that he suddenly needed to leave the town where he'd spent his whole life?

He thought again about boot prints and tire tracks. He could think of no other evidence linking him to the scene. Bending over in quick jabs as he drove, he unlaced his boots.

He stopped before crossing the Yellowstone River at Forsyth and put on his spare boots, the ones too new to walk far in. He sank his old favorites in the river. They were worn out, he thought, and even if they did wash up someplace, they would look like any other trash carried by the river.

Back on the interstate, Keith began to throw his shotgun shells out the window. They all landed in the median ditch, and he only threw one out every mile or two. When the shells were gone, he tore the box into little bits and dropped them out the window. They fluttered in his slipstream, scattering wildly and disappearing. Keith watched them so long he nearly drove off the road. He felt as though it was his whole life he was watching, torn up and blowing away.

He reloaded his gun's magazine with the old kind of shells, with only one shot size. There was no written record anywhere that he had ever owned mixed-shot shells.

As he'd emptied the elastic loops of his vest, his hand brushed over the pocket where he kept his homemade walnut turkey call. It wasn't until he'd reloaded his gun that he realized the pocket was empty.

Tears had been close to Keith's eyes, but when he found that the call was missing, the new jet of fear dried them. He'd been beginning to think he was going to get away with it, though he didn't think "get away with" was the right term. You got away with shady things you wanted to do, though you knew you shouldn't. Keith had never had something go so completely wrong, something that he would have given anything to take back. He might not get caught, he thought, but he would never get away.

He had made the turkey call himself, and immediately he

could think of at least ten people he had shown it to. There were more than that, too. He marveled at how little anonymity there really was in a person's life, even someone as private as himself. He thought of the full turkey mount in his office, and the pictures on his walls of himself, in camouflage, holding up bird after bird after bird. When he had finished making the turkey call, he had left it on his desk, proudly, for people to see.

Keith lifted up in his seat so he could see himself in the rearview mirror. He'd forgotten he was still wearing face paint. He couldn't see a thing about his face, and he wished he could leave the paint on forever. But there wasn't enough camouflage in the world to hide what he had done.

Without hope, he worked over every pocket of his vest and clothing, and there was no call. He remembered how he had been working the plunger when the gobble tore out so close, and he could picture exactly how he had left the call on the ground as he shifted his hand to the round, wooden forearm of his shotgun.

As Keith put both his shaking hands on the steering wheel, it began to snow. It shouldn't be snowing in the spring, either, he thought. But soon he was wishing the snow would never stop, that it would bury everything back by the roost trees.

Keith left the interstate at the tiny town of Custer. It was still only eight o'clock on a Sunday morning, and there was no traffic on the interstate, or in Custer. He was the only customer in the cafe, and he managed to say hello to the waitress on his way to the bathroom.

Keith picked the slim bar of scented soap from the edge of the dirty sink and began to scrub at his face and hands. He did not lift his face until the muddy, green flow of water swirled crystal clear again, pooling over the rust-edged drain hole. His face was pale and shaky in the soap-spotted mirror. He was ashamed that he could still recognize it.

He dried off on the revolving towel roll, went back into the cafe, and sat down. He knew he could not face his wife yet, and he wanted to practice speaking to anyone at all. The first thing the waitress asked was if he'd got one.

"Yep," Keith said, "a little one."

"Where were you hunting?"

Keith managed to give the smile he always gave to that question, and he hid his face behind his coffee cup before the smile began to fall apart.

"There were a couple guys in here real early, filling up thermoses. They were all painted up, too."

"Opening day," Keith said.

"You got it. That's why I opened early. Pretty soon we'll have a crowd. As much a one as we ever get."

He resisted asking what the two men had looked like, and he ordered eggs and hashbrowns that he left untouched half an hour later. "Don't think I'm quite over that flu, yet," he said as he waited for the change. A bell jingled when he opened the door to leave, a bell he hadn't noticed on his way in. The waitress called out for him to have a good day.

The shaking took over again as he left the highway exit to his house. It was just after ten o'clock, and he wondered what he could possibly do for the rest of the day. He might say he was sick. It would not be a lie. His insides were loose, his stomach empty and nauseous.

He pulled into his drive and saw that his wife's car was missing, and he remembered that she and their daughter would be at church. He was thankful for that. He pulled his Blazer into the garage and closed the door behind it. He was taking out his gun when he saw the dead turkey in the back. He'd never before brought home an ungutted bird.

Keith sat on his tailgate and cleaned the turkey. The entrails were cold and sticky, and Keith hated that touch, much more so than the feel of the still hot, fresh bird. He dumped the guts and the few feathers he had plucked into the trash and hung the bird from the usual hook on the rafter. It wasn't the smallest turkey he had ever shot, but close, and he began to make up a story for his wife, who had expected him to return with the giant as fully as he had expected it himself.

He was almost out of the garage when he realized he had not yet tagged the turkey. He took the tag from his pocket and cut out the date, hardly able to picture what would have happened if he'd come across a game check station. He started shaking again.

Once inside his house, Keith began to run a tub for himself. As he undressed he paced the house, which seemed unfamiliar to him now. He threw his hunting clothes into the hamper and stopped, naked, over his stack of hunting magazines. His throat dried up to the point where he thought he would choke, and he wondered if he would be able to clean his shotgun without breaking down.

Keith feigned illness all that day. He lay on the couch watching a baseball game without seeing a single play. He heard the turkeys waking and pictured the gray giving way and giving way, until it was nearly light enough to see. Then he listened to the startled flush, and knew they had spotted the man behind the thicket. He could feel the thin dowel of his hen call's plunger, and he could hear the gobble, now recognizing the just less than authentic wail of it. The flash of red was always there, and the buck of the gun against his shoulder. Tears came near to overflowing his eyes several times, more for all he would lose than for the little man in the thicket. The red of the bandanna mixed with the red of the unbelievable amount of blood scattered across the man's chest and pooled on the ground below his neck. He wanted to scream at the dead man for wearing that red.

His wife came into the television room before dinner, but he shook his head, saying he couldn't eat a thing. It must be the flu, she said, coming on as fast as it had. Then she asked what had happened out there, and Keith found it hard to breathe.

She sat on the couch beside him. "That is one small turkey," she said, smiling, and Keith realized she was only trying to cheer him up.

"Nothing went like I thought it would," he murmured.

"The monster got away?"

"They saw me just lifting the gun. I had him, the big one, but that little one ran in front just as I shot. I couldn't believe it."

"Must be how he got so big," she said, patting his head and heading back for the kitchen. She had never understood his passion, and she was probably glad to have the small bird, which would be tender out of the oven.

The television was on all that evening, but Keith did not hear a word of it. The smaller sounds of his home surrounded him, driving out all else, all except his pictures of the thicket. He listened to Patty and Kim, their eight-year-old, eat dinner. Kim had fought with Brandi, her best friend. Patty told her not to worry, said that those things just happen and they would be best friends again tomorrow.

Their forks clinked, and Keith wondered what they were eating. Patty usually fixed something a little fancy for Sunday night, but he could not place the smell of it. He still smelled pine and juniper and the stale, hot smell of burnt powder.

They cleared the table together after dinner and they talked as they washed, but their voices were drowned by the rush of rinse water and clatter of dishes.

Later Kim snuck into the TV room and peered at her father. He looked up, sensing she was there, and he could not even manage a smile. "Are you awake?" she asked.

Keith nodded, afraid to speak.

"Are you watching this?"

Keith had hardly been aware the TV was on. "No," he said, and his voice sounded normal.

"Mind if I watch my show?"

Keith shook his head, and watched while she turned the stations and settled into the leather chair that was much too big for her. She had red socks on, and they stuck out into the air when she scrunched her butt into the back of the chair.

Tears finally broke through, then, and Keith rolled to the inside of the couch and put an arm over his head. After his wife had put Kim to bed, she sat in the same chair reading, and Keith listened to her turn the pages, thought he could practically hear her lips move the way they did if she didn't catch herself. The leather rustled under her, and he knew she had shifted a leg up under her on the chair. She was probably fiddling with her toes now absentmindedly as the book absorbed her.

It seemed like she read for days, and when he finally heard her leave the chair, he listened to her two soft footsteps in the carpet, and his body tensed before she touched his shoulder. She asked if he was ready to come to bed.

Keith shook his head, but knew he would have to speak. "I can't give this to you," he said. "This is a bad one. I'll stay out here."

They argued gently for a few moments, then she squeezed his shoulder and said goodnight and went to their bedroom at the back of the house. He even heard her back there, brushing her teeth, combing her hair, flushing the toilet. He thought he would go insane if he would never be able to stop hearing so much, but if the sounds stopped he was afraid he would die. His body began to quake again, uncontrollably, and it was dark, dark in his house and he knew he would never sleep.

He did not know how long he had been staring into the darkness when he sat bolt upright on the couch. The house was silent. Totally silent. "Oh my God," Keith said out loud. He was running through the blackened house, as he had down the trail, his feet knowing the route without his eyes to help.

He felt his eardrums might burst they strained so, searching, searching for the slightest trace of their breathing.

He flew into his daughter's room and stopped just before flashing on the light. Her curtains were open, and the streetlights gave a predawn grayness to the room. Kim was on her back, the sheet and blanket tucked tight around her neck. Her mouth gaped open, and Keith reached forward and brushed the line of her jaw. He could hear her breaths now, slow and wonderfully steady. He watched the blankets rise and fall in the same perfect rhythm.

Keith crept out of her room, his skin tingling and his insides taking wild flights of their own. Sweat was trickling down his back and his legs. In his own bedroom, Patty was curled away from him, toward the window where she liked to watch the stars.

He could not see her face, and he did not reach to touch her. He stood listening, and the sound of her breathing seemed strong enough to hold up the walls. Keith stood in the doorway, wondering that his legs could support him, and he tried to suck in the strength of those breaths. Then he turned and walked away.

It was cold outside, and Keith shut the door behind him. He had not thought to take a jacket, but it felt right to have the chill wrap tightly around him, like a blanket that would not work. The streetlights lit odd portions of the blank spring branches of the elms, and Keith tried not to think of the grasping, clawing branches he had run through. The elms had been dying here finally, and Keith wondered if any of them would put out leaves this year.

It truly was cold, and Keith walked all the way to the police station before he realized it was snowing. He wrapped his arms around his chest for warmth and stood in the shadows outside the station, staring at its light spilling onto the white sidewalk.

The snow would hide every trace of his crime, he thought. But the snow would not fall inside him, and it would hide nothing there. Keith stood in the shadows, the snow sifting down around him, and tried to decide.

Blues in the Reefs

I GLANCED TO THE EAST, but my headlights were still the only light, and I wondered again about being out so early. I checked the speedometer and looked at the white square of the upland bird regs pinched between the dash and my coffee cup. I'd read them over yet again while I'd waited for the tank to fill. The daily limits allowed fifteen doves, though I couldn't remember ever having seen more than two in the same day. The regs also allowed eight partridge and five grouse. And though the old man and I had gone entire seasons without bouncing a covey of partridge, and my record low for grouse was two, both taken with a rifle, I knew those were within the realm of possibility—the bright possibilities always aglow before the season's first light. I took a sip of coffee. Eight Huns, five grouse. Opening day. It could happen.

I kept checking my speed, easing off the gas again and again. I laughed a little and rolled the window the rest of the way down. Labor Day weekend, five thirty in the morning, already seventy-five degrees, on its way to a hundred. I told myself again that the temperature was the only reason I was out so early. It wasn't the opener, I thought, it was the heat. I wanted to get the walking done before it became ridiculous. The old man would've laughed himself sick if he'd seen me packing my vest and gun at four thirty in the morning, the coffee just starting to dribble into the pot. I glanced at the dash and eased off the gas.

By the time I pulled off at the lake and wound around its shore on the gravel track, I could go without headlights. I tried to take it easy by the summer homes, but I drove fast enough that I had to keep my eyes tight to the road. Right in the middle of all the houses I saw the birds, and I skidded to a stop just in time, my dust swallowing me from behind. Six or seven Huns picked their way across the road, glaring at me like so many miniature chickens. They reached the ditch and watched unflustered as I crept by, glancing from them to the houses and back. The only houses on the whole road.

When I left the lake I drove into the hills, remembering the year we'd found fifteen Huns standing in the middle of this stretch of road. At every corner I craned my neck, but the Huns weren't there. I couldn't decide if the Huns at the houses were a good omen or bad. I still hadn't figured it out when I pulled over at the sharp bend and shut the engine off.

The day had brightened, although the sun still had a ways to go before clearing the mountains in the east. I smiled again, shaking my head at my shorts and tank top, my long socks rolled back down over the top of my boots. I stuck two water bottles— one water, one ice—in my vest's game pouch. I couldn't remember ever having worn shorts hunting before.

I filled my front pockets with shells, seven and a half shot, and looked back down the bottom I'd driven up. There was too much country here, I thought, though I backtracked immediately—there could never be too much country. But the old man and I had hiked through the long grass of those rolling hills and through the heartbreaking tangle of cottonwood and willow and rose in the bottom, where we could sometimes hear birds breaking out—ruffeds, we guessed—from the cover. But we'd never seen one, let alone gotten off a shot.

We'd bumped into Huns in that open land, and once they were up, there was little better. The coveys flushed along the tails of hills rolled down from the high ground and could be worked again and again. The first rushed shots could be made up for, and we could jump them until our shooting was smooth and we'd taken what we guessed was the covey's limit.

But I knew the Huns appeared only once in every ten or fifteen sweeps, and I didn't have the heart to go through all that land alone. Instead I turned my back to it and started up the steep part, toward where the high ridges were broken by jutting teeth of black stone, what the old man, a navy veteran, used to call The Reefs. That's where the blues would be, could be counted on with something beyond wishes, picking up kinnikinnick and grape and snowberries on the edges, and pine seeds and needles in the thick stuff in the lee of the reefs.

I couldn't quite give up on the Huns, though, and as I headed up I walked through the bits of cover, low juniper and scrub, with my shotgun at the ready. But nothing rose, and pretty soon I was into the huffing part, picking my way up the loose rock, taking time to rest crouched with a hand on my knee, the lake more jewel-like the farther it fell away. My white socks had already turned the color of the grass, stuck full of sharp seeds. I took a drink from my unfrozen bottle and wiped the sweat away from my forehead. The sun would be on me soon, and I began to climb again, wanting to be up top before the heat beat me down.

The next time I stopped to blow I was on the edge of the first saddle, a small hollow holding a loose knot of pines. I waited until my breath was back, then I held it and crept through the trees, waiting for the grouse to explode out of the ground around me.

But no grouse came by the time I crossed through the timber, and I pushed hard up the last steep part, leaving the sharp scent of the trees for the dry, dusty smell of the grass. When I cleared the ridge top I was in the sun, and I sat down to take another drink. Now I'd hold the ridges, the grouse's realm, the hard part over.

The grass here was short, inches short, as if sanded off by wind. I looked back down at all the rich country below, and though I knew better, I had the familiar feeling that I'd tricked myself into working the barren land, leaving the most productive area behind. I wiped the sweat away again, checked my shells and pocketed my water bottle, empty now, and started to walk.

I hadn't gone six feet when I saw the blue. He was standing a foot below the ridge, on a broken chunk of granite, watching me, already fidgety, bobbing his weight back and forth from one foot to the other. I glanced quickly around, saw an avenue through the trees I wished he'd take, and I moved back a step, to leave the lane open. The grouse ducked again but didn't take off.

I lifted my gun half up, fingering the thumb safety, wishing the grouse had just blown up when he saw me. I always did better that way, before I had time to think. But I knew this time to collect myself was a gift for the first bird of the season, and as I glanced again at the open slot through the trees, the grouse launched up, wings clattering, and I raised my gun the rest of the way.

He followed the slot and I pulled the trigger, too fast the first time, just like always. I barely saw his tail flare at the shot, and I followed him like I knew I should and the second shot knocked him tumbling to the rockslide that had cleared the path through the trees.

I pulled my empties and reloaded, knowing the blues usually hung in coveys, but as I picked my way down to him nothing else came up. I sat on a rock like a chair and smoothed the first bird of the year out on my lap. Its tail was wide, dull and dark, the flash of orange above its eye startlingly bright.

I climbed back to the ridge with the grouse and sat down in the sun before it grew unbearable. I gutted the bird quickly against the heat and slipped it into my pouch beside the ice bottle. I wiped my fingers in the brittle stems of grass and knew that even if I saw no others, this morning was a success. Even in the reefs there was no guarantee. There'd been plenty of times when the old man and I had walked through here with nothing but ourselves for company. He would've teased me hard about that first shot, the rushed one, though I'd seen him do the same thing often enough.

I checked my shells again, a habit of his I couldn't break, and I followed the ridge until it dropped off sharply. I swung north again, through a long, grassy rise toward the next ridge. But it was a false ridge, the next real one farther back behind it, and I stood looking up its rocky spine, a classic reef. I took my first step up toward it, when I caught the movement in the bottom.

It happened too fast to be sure, but it had, for an instant, looked like grouse, two or three, set-winged, settling down into the snowberry scrub in the bottom of the bowl. That was a half mile off, and I wondered if they weren't really robins, flitting around, and I stood a long time to see if they might not make another flight. The longer nothing rose the surer I was that they were grouse, out of the trees for the first time in the morning, flying to the feeding grounds. I couldn't remember ever having seen a grouse fly in anything but their wild flushes, and I smiled, thinking of them flying like geese to their feed. It made me doubt that they were really grouse, but I started down to see just exactly what I had seen.

I marked them carefully by a lone snag and clump of boulders, and I dropped back into the shade of the ridge as I neared the spot. Nothing happened, and I began to think I'd been fooled by a flight of robins. But then a big blue burst out from the base of the snag, starting with the crazy headlong rush down the draw, before setting his wings and curving away and back up to land on the spine of the ridge, in a clear stretch of grass long enough that the sun was touching its tips, the one golden spot on the dark face of the reef.

I'd crouched at the flush, gun rising before I'd seen it was out of range. Then I took a step forward, and two more burst out from below me, again out of range, and I began to wonder what I had stumbled upon. I turned down the hill, and a whole group launched up, five or six of the big birds, again too far away. I fired anyway, wasting two shots, too excited not to.

The shots shook the rest out, some closer, in range, where I had to watch, gun empty, as they swung down and arced back up, all somehow following the leader into the golden patch of sunlight.

I swore and laughed and reloaded, imagining the old man really giving it to me now, dumping my shots at the hopeless while the possible escaped so cleanly. A whole fleet, he would've called it, and I didn't have a bird. Standing in the cool shade, I squinted against the brightness of the grouse's new cover, marking with care each spot I'd seen the birds settle into. I saw how I would climb the ridge, swinging wide to avoid flushing them early, how I would follow the ridge down, the sun at my back, that sparkling grass marking where the grouse would come up, scattered now, flushing in singles or pairs.

They would head for the draw, setting their wings and sailing, bright in the sun while the land I'd just crossed lay dark below them, still hidden in the shadow of the reef, leaving me and danger a half mile behind with only those few shockingly strong, fast beats of their wings.

And I pictured too how open the land was, how nothing could get in my way, how much time I would have to swing with the birds in those golden seconds of sunlight, how they would tumble with the shot, back down to shadow, and how I would stare after them, wondering what I had done, wondering what I had ever done to deserve this.

I began the stiff walk up to the top of the reef, and when I crested its rocky lip, I wiped the sweat from my face and opened my gun and checked my shells. Then I turned back down to the stretch of sun and grass, and I started off to open my first season without the old man, the sun strong against my back, the grouse scattered and waiting before me.

Grayfish

THE FIRE ATE QUICKLY through the crusted layer of old snow, smudging the dingy edges with black. Some of the pine Marty and John threw on was heavy with resin, and pitchy smoke swept upward. They kept throwing more wood onto the stack because they were wet and cold and there was no end to the wood. Soon tongues of fire shot up taller than the two men. They laughed at the flames' wildness, then fell quiet, staring into the heart of the beguiling tempest.

A long, twisted sheet of birch bark at the edge of the fire, where the snow had been shortly before, began to writhe, and the men watched it curl tighter and tighter and then begin to unfold again. Its inside, the side that had wrapped against the tender parts of the tree, ignited, and the white bark on the outside began to brown. Marty said it looked like a marshmallow ready to come out. But then an old weakness, a knothole maybe, gave way, and a mouth opened in the bark and widened, stretching hideously, as if in silent ululation. Fire belched forth. The bark was engulfed then, and hard to see, and Marty did not say anything else for some time.

Steam began to rise from their pants, and they turned around and stood letting their rears toast. Marty said they should be on spits. He looked over at John, and John looked back and smiled. Talking was a habit with Marty—was with most people. Even up here alone with his brother, he continued to talk. Some habits were harder to break than others, and Marty figured it didn't hurt anything.

When the last batch of wood they'd thrown on began to truly burn, it was too hot to stand near the fire, and they shuffled down the brief strip of broken rock to the lake's shoreline. Thin, fragile ice extended a foot or two out over the water, and just beyond that the young grayling patroled, their big fins down, their blue spots muted by the gray of the sky.

This wasn't Alaska, not true grayling country, but down in the lower states, the last remnants of a forgotten stocking effort. The lake itself was high and out of the way. The fish had reproduced unchecked, until they choked the lake with this ring of marauding dwarfs. But bigger fish were out there. The record in this state was something over seventeen inches, and they caught several larger than that every year. Especially in the spring, if they caught the ice-out right. But if they'd turned in the records, they'd have had to say where they were caught. Marty could get John worked into a silent furor just teasing about turning in one of the monsters for a record.

This morning, after the long, soggy hike through snow still deep in the draws, and after the long wondering if the lake was open yet, they had crested the last ridge and seen the sheen of open water. With that driving away the cold, they had set up their rods and gone after them, same as every year, content to slaughter the smaller fish, thinking there was something the two of them could do in the way of population control.

Just as the cold was returning, though, nagging for the fire, Marty had reared back and launched an unusually long cast. John had been working shorter and shorter, rather than reaching out to push the ice out of the guides. He stopped and watched Marty, timing the drop of the weighted nymph. Marty began the hopping retrieve exactly the same time as he would have, and John gave a low, grunting whoop and shook his fist. His brother turned and smiled at the same time the fish hit, and as soon as John saw how the rod bowed, he came barreling down the beach to see if he could help.

But the grayling gave up easily, as they did now and then, and by the time John was there, Marty had it sidling in, first running right, then running left. Its ridiculous, gorgeous fin was spread wide, fighting the pull, and the blood surge of the fight brightened its red and blue spots as if the fish itself were alight.

Marty had to break a channel through the thin shore ice with his boot. Then, when he took the fish carefully from the water, they held it against John's rod. Marty flattened the tail down and evened it with the cork butt. The fish's small, jutting mouth stopped about an inch past the nick that marked the state record but was short of John's personal nick—his personal world record nick. A quarter inch short.

John gave another of his deep, whooping roars and slapped Marty on the back. Marty bent over the water again, hands in the icy lake, reviving the strangely fragile fish. John's last rough slap nearly tipped him over, and he let go of the fish to put out his arm to stop his fall. The fish darted down the steep drop into the black heart of the lake, as if it had only feigned weakness. Marty was laughing by then, too, and he realized John had kept up his demented whooping. It echoed back from the rock and snow and timber until it had surrounded the lake with the sound of victory.

The old mark on the rod, the longest one, was ten years old now, a fluke, Marty always said. But John held by it, and each fish Marty challenged with that fell short only pleased him that much more. For years Marty had wanted to see one of his fish's rubbery lips eclipse that mark, but they had always fallen just that much short.

After Marty had released the fish, they'd moved up the shoreline and started the fire. Always before they had simply built a small, warming fire, but John was still wound up about the big fish, and he had been the one to go farther into the trees, bringing back the logs. Soon they were trying to outdo each other, until the pyre took on a life of its own and drove them back down to the water.

They chipped the ice from the line guides and started around the lake to the willow thicket at the outlet. John slipped on the ice once, going all the way down, twisting to land on his butt, holding his rod high, away from danger. Marty turned to see if he was all right, and John was smiling hard and pulling himself up. Then Marty started to laugh, pointing, and finally pulling on John's beard, the tip of which was curled and shortened from the heat of the fire. "You burned your beard!" he said, laughing.

John did not understand him, and Marty tugged harder on his beard, trying to pull it around for John to see. John winced and slapped Marty's arm away. Marty went through the necessary pantomime then, and John's face lit up, and he began tugging at his beard himself, feeling the thick, coarse patch of burned hair. He laughed, and Marty wondered how it was that laughing was the only normal sound he could make. It was fitting—he was always laughing—but still Marty wondered. He knew he was the only one who ever heard the wild, excited shouting. Their parents had convinced John early on that the shouting scared people and that he shouldn't do it. But out in the mountains, even as kids, Marty had worked against that training, until John had begun to shout simply for the reaction it caused in his brother. At least that's what Marty figured. Deaf as a stone from birth, there was no other reason he could see for John to shout.

The pantomime reminded Marty of the first time up here, when they had cast out their flies without knowing what lay below the surface. The little grayling were ferocious, and John landed the first one while Marty was still setting up his rod. He'd carried it over, with the Question Look on his face.

Marty had just returned from Alaska, where he'd been working on a crab boat, which, he was to say later, was proof of just how young and dumb a person could be. The grayling surprised him, but he knew they had stocked everything up here at one time or another. But his mind had drawn a blank on the name. Gray something, gray something. John shook the fish under his nose, wanting an identification.

Marty had squatted then, and wrote "Gray" in the sand with his finger. Then he pounded his fist against the shore, and looked up at John and shook his head. John squatted beside him just as Marty wrote "Grayfish." He knew that wasn't right. He was thinking out loud.

Then John's hand swept across the sand, obliterating the word. His laughter pealed across the lake. First he wrote "Moron," with an arrow pointing to Marty. Marty laughed a little, but though he'd been away for a year, he still recalled all the times he'd heard kids shouting that word, and he did not look at John. The next word John wrote was "Grayling."

Marty laughed. "That's it! I knew that."

When John wrote, "Which one of us was in Alaska?" the name of Grayfish Lake had been sealed. Later, when Marty was working shrimp on the Texas gulf coast, John had sent him a cutout of a grayling, made of gray construction paper. On the back side was written, "Grayfish (Fishus grayus)." There was nothing else in the envelope, and Marty had laughed until he nearly cried.

Now they walked toward the willows again, more carefully on the ice, because Grayfish really was a place far enough away, and high enough up, that even a sprain could mean bad things.

Marty parted the first of the branches, and the raft was still there. They dragged it out together, sweating before they were through, although the logs seemed dry and buoyant once they edged them into the lake. Ten years ago they'd brought up the rope and lashed the dead lodgepoles together, pushing the platform out into the lake wondering if they were just going for a quick swim. They hadn't even had the paddles then, and Marty doubted there was ever a less stable craft built. But they'd eased it past the band of stunted fish, out into deeper and deeper water, where there was no bottom, and where the big rises ringed the water sporadically. That was when the record breakers really started to fall.

Since then the raft had been modified. One year an outrigger had been added, and the next, in the greatest innovation, they'd dumped the outrigger in favor of a double raft, a kind of catamaran, with a raised floor of thin pine poles. It still steered like a bathtub, but it kept them more or less out of the water, and they could both cast at once if they were careful.

And they were always careful. Today, Marty knew, with the low, constant layer of cloud, and the ice girdling the lake, a dump in deep water might be the end of things, even before shore, and the fire, could be reached. He'd seen a young hand go over the side of a crabber off the Aleutians. He'd been blue and stiff before he could be retrieved, and he never did make it back.

Marty grabbed John's arm and pointed at the ice and the clouds and the water. He made the Careful Sign then, and John nodded and they pushed off, digging the frayed ends of their canoe paddles against the frozen sand ripples on the bottom until their raft was free.

There was nothing fancy involved. They simply paddled straight out, until the bottom was gone, and then a little farther. Maybe one hundred yards. They'd explored the lake before, and the raft was beached off the most productive spot, though it had been a toss-up, one place seemingly as good as the next.

They started stripping line out together, and John saw the first rise, off to the left, followed a moment later by a second, coming closer. Neither one of them could see what the fish might be rising to, but these were the least particular fish they'd ever known. They both left on their small weighted hare's ears, and John dropped his past and in front of the path of rises.

He hooked up immediately, and the fish did not give up as Marty's had. John was as silent as ever while the fight was on, and Marty, guessing the fish would be close to that final nick, watched John's eyes, quick and alert where they followed the cut of the line through the burnished surface of the lake. He grinned again at the singed beard, and the flaps of his woolen cap dangling foolishly over the useless ears.

Marty took his net from over his shoulder, but John waved him away. He netted the fish himself, swiftly, before it was worn down. He held his rod down to the water, and gave a quiet grunt, releasing the grayling without lifting it from the lake. He smiled then, looking at Marty and holding his thumb and index finger a half inch apart. That much short. His fingertips were red where they poked through the sodden wool of his fingerless gloves. He wouldn't even show Marty the fish unless it broke at least the state record.

The raft circled slowly in a breeze that hardly marred the surface of the lake. Marty caught a little fish, the size of the young marauders. He held it up and shouted at it, asking what the hell it was doing out in the middle of the lake, and his words, along with John's laughing, echoed across the lake. He killed the fish to add to the stringer they would have for dinner and wedged it in a crack between two of the decking logs.

The cloud covering the sky eased down until the mountains disappeared, and the trees rising up their flanks blended into a foggy graygreen. The lake turned even darker, nearly black, smooth as a slate. Tiny globes of the mist beaded onto the hairs of their clothing until they glistened. Anywhere they touched broke the beads and the cloth turned dark and wet before more mist pearled up.

Even the breeze died as the lake socked in, and the raft stopped its slow twist. It left Marty facing the shore, where the fire still burned steadily, though with less manic ferocity. As he watched, a pulsing red ring formed around the fire, surging out, falling back, and surging forth again, a trick of flame and moisture. Marty stared at it, forgetting to fish, and when he reached across their frail raft and tugged on John's arm, he did not know that John was bringing in a fish.

He turned when John jerked his arm away, and then tugged again. John looked over his shoulder, annoyed, but when he saw the fire and its ring the scowl dropped away from his face and he sat and stared. The awed smile stole so slowly over his features that Marty didn't see it form. Then the ring wavered and winked out. Although they looked for a minute or two longer, the halo did not return.

Then John was tugging at Marty's arm, holding up another grayling and his fingers again, showing it was just shy of the all-time world record. Marty smiled slowly, then waved his hand, dismissing the fish. He slapped himself on the chest, saying his was much bigger than that, and John laughed and let the fish go. Marty listened to the laugh, imagining it as a pulsing glory around his brother, and he stripped in his line for another cast.

The fishing out deep was slower than the frantic hookings of the smaller fish near shore, but the fish were all big, except for the midget Marty'd killed. It was near dusk, and they were both wet again, from the mist, and the fire had settled down to little more than a glow. They'd each landed several fish near record size, but none as close as Marty had come from shore. Marty tapped John, pointed at his wrist and the fire, and nodded his head toward shore.

John agreed and held up his finger in the traditional Last-Cast Sign. This was the contest of them all, and Marty stripped out all the line he could possibly cast, giving himself that much more chance. He'd always been able to cast farther than his brother, and when their lines touched down, he made faces at John, showing him what he thought of such a tiny cast. John smiled back and gave him the finger.

John hooked up first. It looked like a big fish, and he started his war whoop for the first time since Marty had landed the fish from shore. He fought the fish carefully, but his face was lit up, facing Marty, taunting him. He whooped again and the dew shook away from his beard.

It really was an ugly noise, that whoop, and Marty knew his parents were right. It would scare people. But he laughed back at his brother and turned to his own line. He'd let it sink too deep, and when he jigged his rod tip, the strike was so solid he thought he might have embedded the nymph in an ancient drowned tree. But then his line was off and running, and in the moment when he still had time, he lunged across the raft to slap John, to show him what he had. He saw John's face, stunned and not smiling for an instant before he heard the whooping blurt out again and again, as if the lid had been jarred loose from some long-buried torment.

The fish turned before Marty tightened up on him, and he quartered, keeping the line tight, testing its pull. Then it broke away again, ticking line off the reel, and by the cut of the line he knew the fish was changing depths, coming up, seeing if that would free him. Marty wondered how long it'd been since the fish had left the murky depths he'd let his fly sink to.

The fish did not break the surface before it turned again, coming in on Marty, and he stripped line back. He'd never seen anything but grayling come from this lake, but this fish fought with experience and power that he had never felt in any of the grayling before.

It was still down deep when it went under the raft, on John's side. Marty leapt that way, passing his rod to John, who gave a startled grunt as the raft tipped crazily down. He took the rod from Marty and passed it under his, which was still bucking with his fish. John's eyes went wide in the moment he touched the rod, and he gave it back to Marty, his mouth slack, grinning.

Marty crab-crawled back to his side of the raft, and the fish seemed to just give up. It was holding sideways again, like the fish in the morning—the famous grayling trick of spreading its prehistoric fin, making the fisherman drag it through the water if he could. He glanced at John, wondering what he could have transmitted through the rod to this fish, to make it give in so easily.

John was netting his fish just then. Marty saw the rod go down, and he saw the smile again. Then Marty glanced back to his line, its yellow curve having a little belly back in it as the fish came in with less and less resistance.

Then, just beyond the end of the yellow stripe in the black water, the fish appeared, still holding sideways, every fin flared as widely as possible, the bright shocks of color burning holes through the darkness of the lake. The body, bowed away from the pull, was long and broad, a gargantuan unlike any they had ever pulled from the lake.

It shook once, weakly, and just at the edge of his vision Marty could see John with his fish out of the water, pinned against the deck, measuring it carefully against his rod. He saw the intensity in his brother's face, the precision of the judging. Then, still holding the fish down, staring at it, John began the first of his whoops. He lifted his head back, eyes closed, and howled his whoops out.

Marty tore back on his rod. He saw the fish jerk through the water and fight again, pulling away, and Marty ripped back one more time. He felt the line part, and he saw the fish start backward, then stop and hang motionless for an instant before its own muscles took over and it was gone with one flash of color.

Marty did not take the time to stare at where it had disappeared, but he slammed his rod down and started to swear. But he was not listening to himself. He was listening to that frightening cry, rebounding through the cirque that imprisoned the lake, ringing them in their ridiculous, dangerous raft as surely as the ghostly corona had ringed the fire.

He turned then to John, who had just seen that Marty had lost the fish and was laughing too hard to keep whooping. He pointed at his fish, and Marty crawled carefully to where John had it pinned against the rod, its lip just touching their world record mark.

Marty shook his head as if he was disappointed and pointed at the water where his fish had disappeared. He held his hands up, a good two feet apart, and John had tears running from his eyes, down to his singed beard, and he nodded his head vigorously, shaking his finger at the same spot in the water, his mouth gaping with laughter. Marty could hear the scream inside his brother's head, "That's right! That's right! That's exactly where your fish is! In the lake!"

Marty waved his brother's laughing away, and picking up his paddle, he started for shore while John revived his fish and released it to the lake. But it was hopeless without John paddling to balance his effort, so Marty stopped.

He watched his brother's back hunched over the black water, the dew still glistening off his coat. He'd broken the fish off purposely, out of pity, and Marty hated himself for that. John had never pitied himself a day in his life. Marty'd once, a long time ago, told John that he would give him his ears, if he could. It was a stupid, useless thing to say, and John had just smiled and written, "Who'd want those car doors?"

John straightened on his side of the raft after the fish had stirred and shot away, and Marty swatted him with his paddle and pointed to shore. He turned forward then, away from his brother, but he thought he could still hear the dying quaver of John's victory cry, rippling through the cirque like a haunting.

First Time Out

SHEENA AND I WERE DRIVING back to Great Falls, bypassing the best ring of potholes I know, when, out of force of habit, I asked her if she'd like to see if any ducks were around. It was a warm day, the sun brilliant on the snow-heavy mountains surrounding the valley, and she said, "Sure."

You don't know Sheena, so that hardly comes as a shock. But it caught me a little off guard. Every year I'd buy her a bird license and a duck stamp, and I always carried around both shotguns, but when I popped the question it was a second before I realized what she'd said. I nearly missed the turn.

We bumped down the dirt road, and when I parked she asked, "They're just over that hill?"

She meant the ponds, and I said that was right. I put on my waders, changed into a gray-brown shirt, and tossed another shirt to her. It was kind of a nondescript brown-green and she looked at it.

"It's for camouflage," I said.

"I thought you said all we had to do was walk up to the edge of the pond and shoot them."

"Yeah, but you can't let them see you before then."

She put on the shirt and asked what the waders were for.

"Retrieving," I said. I only had one pair of waders.

I had two shotguns, both double-barrels of no particular value, and I gave her the down and dirty about loading and swinging through the target and a lot about safety. Never point it unless you mean to shoot, always expect it to go off—that kind of thing.

Once she'd crawled under the fence, I handed her the guns. I followed her under, and we started up through the sagebrush for the first pond. I was excited that she was finally giving it a chance, and I kept on telling her how it'd be and what we would do. She knows how I get, and she let me go on for quite a while before asking me to be quiet.

Ever since we've known each other, Sheena's understood about the fall. Never once complained, but never got too excited about joining me. There wasn't any of that sneaking out the back door with the gun case, or whining about the old lady not letting me go hunting. She loves to let me go hunting.

Occasionally I'll hunt with a group of guys she works with, and if the hunting gets hot, there's always the rush to town for the calls to the wives, asking if they can stay out an extra day, or even two. I always get a kick out of that. I wait for the phone booth to clear before I call Sheena and ask if it would be all right if I came home in a day or two. She usually lets me, though now and then she asks if I wouldn't like to stay out longer.

I was trying to tell Sheena how much I appreciated that, but we were both blowing pretty hard from the climb, and it wasn't easy talking. She didn't say anything back.

We made the top of the hill, after a couple of breathers, and I could see the pond glinting away out there in the distance. It was hard to see the water though, because of all the ducks. I passed the binoculars to Sheena so she could see, but she only said, "I thought you said it was just over the hill."

I nodded. "Now we drop down this gully and keep that little ridge between the pond and us."

We rested a little, but you never know when they're going to fly off someplace, so we pushed on. Even walking hunched over to keep our heads out of view, the going was faster than the uphill. We reached the end of the ridge pretty quick.

I turned around and whispered that the pond was right over there now. You could see the tops of the cattails. We had to crawl from here, and I showed her how to cradle the gun to keep it from scraping on the ground.

"What do you mean crawl?" she asked.

"Just to the cattails. Here, we better load up. If we spook them early, we might still have a shot."

I passed two of the #4 magnums back to her, and she loaded like a pro. She even smiled at the click the barrels made when they closed, although she was looking at me. I smiled back, and we started to crawl.

For the first stretch there's still the sage, and I kind of wove through that, keeping the biggest clumps between me and the pond. There's a little prickly pear in there, too, but it's easy enough to miss. I stopped once to rest, and after I asked she whispered back that she hadn't hit any cactus after the first bunch. She wanted to know if it was time to shoot yet.

I tried not to smile. I shook my head and pointed at the cattails. "Not till there." I started crawling again.

In a little while we were out of the sage and into the pond grass. We'd stopped a few times to rest, and I'd heard some commotion from the far end of the pond, quacking and splashing, so I veered that way a little. Water started to soak through the forearm of my shirt, where my arm held my weight and the shotgun. It wasn't much, though.

I turned around when Sheena grabbed my ankle. I looked into the barrels of her shotgun, pointing right up my rear end. I pushed them away, reminding her that she had to think the gun could go off at any time. She said she had been. Then she said, "You said it was going to be dry."

"Practically."

She pushed her hand down into the grass in front of her and brown water welled up. I looked down at my own knees and saw the same brown water pooled around the rubber of my waders. The thighs of her jeans had turned that wet, shiny, blue, with tan seed heads stuck all over. "We're almost there," I said.

She shook her head and motioned me forward.

I got a lot closer than I thought I would. We were right on the edge of the reeds, and we could even see the ducks a little by looking through the tangle. I motioned that we should head into the cattails and keep going until the ducks jumped. Sheena shook her head. Her gun was pointed at my rear again and I gave her a dirty look and pushed it away. My look was nothing compared to hers.

"Side by side now," I whispered. "Right at them till they jump."

"Right at them is right into the pond."

"You can't ever get too close."

"I can. I am."

"Come on."

"I am not going to crawl into a pond on purpose."

The ducks solved that problem for us. They'd been getting more and more suspicious, and finally they just couldn't stand it. They erupted off the water, and a big group, at least a dozen or so, flew cattail height right at us.

For me that's the toughest target. I launched my first shot too fast and didn't even turn the ducks. I was a little more collected for the second and nearly got one. Sheena didn't shoot.

For almost a minute afterward there were ducks circling everywhere and late ones getting off with the shots and dumb ones trying to put back down. I hid in the reeds, trying to get

Sheena's attention, but she just sat out in the open, watching. With her out there like that, nothing came close enough for a second try. When we were alone again, I said, "A lot of times you'll get another chance. You should have jumped in here, too. They can see you out there."

Sheena said nothing was going to make her jump into a pond. Nothing. I didn't see what difference it'd make, she was pretty much soaked already, but I didn't bring that up. I asked her why she hadn't shot.

"Because all I could see was your humongous head."

"I told you we had to go in side by side, so that wouldn't happen."

"Well, we didn't."

True enough. I walked farther into the reeds and kicked around some, just in case something hadn't gotten up. Really, I was giving her a little cool-off period. It's one of my tricks with her. There were two more ponds pretty close by, and I didn't want her to get mad now.

I was pretty well worn out fighting the reeds and the muck and the water before I came back to shore and told Sheena where the next pond was.

She stared at me for a second and asked if I was serious. I smiled and said sure I was. Then she asked if I'd lost my mind.

I wished I'd hit one of those ducks. She loves eating them, and just having one might have cheered her up. The plucking would've given her a little more cool-off time too.

But I had another idea. I remembered the first time I'd hit anything with a shotgun—a can on a fence post. When that can took off for the next field I was hooked. Same thing could work for Sheena—you never know—so I suggested that she at least try shooting the gun, as long as she'd come all the way out here.

She wasn't too fired up about the idea, but pretty soon we made a deal. If she just tried it, shooting at a tussock out at mid-pond, we would go home without jumping the other ponds. I pictured the rip of white water around the tussock and her surprise that she'd hit it so well, and figured it was at least fifty-fifty whether she'd go to the other ponds after that.

I gave her another round of instructions. "Hold it tight, pull it into your shoulder so it can't slap you. Hold the forearm tight so it won't pull up. Cheek against the stock, eye down the flat of the barrels. Gentle squeeze." All that kind of talk, all overkill because it was the first time. Finally she told me to shut up and get out of the way.

I stepped to the side and watched her set herself up. She's left-handed, so nothing seemed to look that good to me. I was trying to figure out what she was doing wrong when she just seemed to disappear behind the roar of the shotgun.

Ever notice how really loud noises will make your eyes water? It's true. They make fire alarms that loud so even deaf people know something's going on—it makes their eyes water. I couldn't see Sheena till I wiped my eyes.

She was standing a few feet back from where I'd last seen her, and instead of pointing forward, the shotgun was pointing straight up to heaven. She was still pulling it tight to her shoulder, though. Something had gone wrong, but I hadn't yet quite figured out what, so I just said, "You've got to grip that forearm tight, too."

Her ears must've been ringing pretty bad, but by the way her face twisted I could tell she heard me. Then it dawned on me what had happened, and I wished I hadn't said that. She was still just standing there, with the gun pointing at the sky, and I stepped toward her to see if she was all right.

I'd given her the newer gun, the one with the single trigger, because I figured it'd be easier for her. Three times in its career it'd fired both barrels at once. I took it to a gunsmith and he said there was nothing wrong with it. Sometimes those single triggers just did that, he said. But I hadn't been thinking of that when I gave it to her. Didn't even remember it. If I'd been thinking at all, I would have given her a couple of lighter loads.

Sheena wears those big, roundish glasses that got so popular. Makes her look like an owl. Smart, sort of. You know how people who always wear glasses look when you see them without the glasses? Kind of squinty and molish? That's how Sheena looked, but I figured it was the way her eyes were watering that did that. I didn't notice right away about the glasses.

I peeled the shotgun off her shoulder, and that seemed to bring her back to life some. "You said it'd kick a little bit." She said that with the "little" underlined.

"I think I know what happened." I broke the shotgun open, and sure enough there were two neat, little dimples, one in each primer. "It shot both barrels at once. It's not supposed to."

"Why did it?"

"They just do sometimes, I guess."

I was still holding the shotgun up for her to see the spent shells. "See? Both the hammers fell. From the concussion probably." I was trying to remember what the gunsmith had said.

Sheena was wiping at her eyes. "I think my shoulder's broken," she said.

"Oh, it is not. That can't break your shoulder." I laughed a little. "I bet it stung, though."

Even with those moley-looking eyes she gave me one of her looks. She didn't think this was very funny.

"Where are my glasses?" she asked. "Blew my glasses right off my face."

We started looking around in the long grass for her glasses. She couldn't see a thing, but I found them pretty quick. They were easy enough to see right there in my footprint like that. I'd stepped on them when I jumped over to see if she was all right.

I explained that to her, that I'd been worried about her, before I let her have them back. There was still one good lens.

She put the glasses on and she kept staring at me, one eye so big and mean, the other all squinty and evil looking. "'You've got to hold the forearm tight, too,'" she said, mimicking my voice the way she does. Not very flattering. Then she said, "I'll meet you at the car." She said that hard and low, and she turned and started back through the sage.

I knew the other ponds were out of the question. I wasn't even thinking about that. But I hated to see her pissed off and mad and quitting so easily. I chased after her, carrying both the guns, my waders flapping around my chest like giant fish lips.

"Sheena?" I said. I pulled up alongside her and said it again. "Sheena?"

She didn't look at me. With either eye.

"Sheena? You know what they say about falling off a horse. You got to get right back on."

She did stop, then. She turned to me and asked me what they said about a horse's ass.

I didn't know that one. She started marching again.

"I've got some really light shells. Ones that'll hardly kick at all. We'll only put one in. That way it can't do that again. You really ought to get right back on that horse." I was starting to run again, trying to keep up.

She stopped dead in her tracks and I ran into her, but when she looked at me with both those eyes I put a little distance between us.

"You've got lighter shells?" she asked. "Ones that don't kick back like the ones you gave me?"

I saw what was coming but I admitted it anyway, before I could come up with a better answer.

She plucked the shotgun from my hand before I could jerk it

away. "Give me a shell," she said, real slow and cool. "Give me two. And not those little ones. Give me the big ones, the same as you gave me before."

She was facing me squarely, the gun open, her hand out for the shells. I was suddenly pretty glad I had all the shells with me. I told her she should give her shoulder a rest, and I started for the car.

Pretty soon I was at a dead sprint, the waders gumming at me like a carp trying to swallow me whole. But Sheena's got legs halfway to her ears and she wasn't losing a stride.

She just kept waving that shotgun and screaming, "Give me two of the big ones!"

I haven't bought her a duck stamp since.

Flyways

MY MOM MOVED TO CALIFORNIA when I was seven, and I went
with her, of course. In those days the kid always went with the
mother. I missed my dad pretty bad at first, and I missed
Montana. I missed the winter there, and the long stretches of
wheat broken by the worn-out rock ridges and the scrub, and I
missed all the sky. You could walk through that empty land with
only the birds blowing up out of it now and then, holding your
eye until they disappeared. California didn't have anything to
touch that. Up north of San Francisco, where we lived, the
mountains seemed crumbly and black-green and wet, always
pushing you into the ocean. Hardly seemed as if they left enough
room for air.

I'd visit my dad, of course, but even that far apart my folks
kept at each other, and I could only visit once a year. We made
the visits in the fall, my dad and I, so we could spend all our
time out in the open, chasing the birds.

The first time he let me carry a gun I was around ten or
eleven years old. He woke me up in the dark, like he always did,

by wiggling my toe through the blankets. We always got up early when we were together, but it was hard to get used to again. I sat at the table, and I still had stuff in the corners of my eyes and I could feel my hair sticking around in the air. There was frost on the windows, and I shivered a little. It made my hair shake. He kidded me about that and I laughed. He could always make me laugh, but somehow, just being up early in his cold house with the whole frosted world waiting outside for us, I felt I could have laughed for nothing.

He handed me a bowl of oatmeal and picked me up, chair and all, and moved me over next to the stove. It heated my clothes right up, and it was good to feel them against my skin. My dad left the room then, and I was scraping the last raisin out of my bowl before he came back. He had two shotguns with him, and he'd only ever had one before. He took my bowl away from me and put one of the guns across my knees, not letting go of it himself until he saw I had both my hands on it.

I'd seen his guns in his cabinet for years, but until that one was given to me, for me to use, I'd never known what they really were. I held this one against my knees in the yellowy light, with the day still black beyond the frost-rimed window.

It had two barrels, long ones, one next to the other. They tapered as they ran out. There was a tiny bead at the end, in between the barrels. It was the same color as the light. The wood was dark, but I could see darker parts in it yet, and the grain took a big swirl right where the bend is, before it widens out to fit on your shoulder. I traced my finger around the swirl, then picked the gun up to look at it closer. There was a name on it, on the metal—Lefever. It was a perfect name. It made me think of whoever'd made this gun, burning up with it inside him, until he'd gotten it out as perfect as he had. I said the name out loud.

My dad reached down, not taking it away from me, but just

pushing the lever on the top, so the barrels dropped open. I held it up to the light, then, close to my face. The inside of the barrels was smooth, like mirrors, and with it that close I could smell the smell of my dad's hands.

"You're old enough now. That's yours," he said, and I kept staring at it.

"Pretty soon you're going to have to be old enough for everything," he added. I still couldn't believe he had given it to me, and I ran my hand the length of the barrels. Then he said it was time to go, and I stood up and followed him out the door, as if sucked along by his draft.

It wasn't light out yet and the cold pinched my nose shut, but I barely noticed that. The gun was heavy, and it pressed my mittens against my hands. We started to walk to the river, the snow crunching under our feet, crusty with the cold. "They'll all be on the river," my dad said. "The cold snap's got the ponds frozen."

I nodded in the dark like I knew, and started to point the shotgun at things we walked by, from the hip, like they do on TV. He must've seen that. He said, "There's nothing in that gun. It's not loaded."

I stopped pointing it then.

"When you show me you're not going to kill me, I'll give you some shells."

That was my dad. He'd do something like giving me that gun, then feel funny about it, like something had almost surfaced in him, and he was quick going to sink it again. I didn't say anything, but I wished he didn't have to be like that. Then he said, "Don't point it unless you're going to shoot. Ever."

I tried to hold it without pointing it then, but it did have barrels and they had to point somewhere. By the time we reached where we had to crawl to his blind, it seemed like it pointed everywhere at once. When we got in, I sat on the cold bench and held the gun in my lap again, with the barrels pointed away from my dad. He did the same on his side of the bench.

It was getting light enough to see, but nothing happened. I began blowing my breath onto my mittens, watching the frost stick on the end of each little wool hair. The honking sounded so far away it took a second to sink in, then I lifted my head because it seemed like something I couldn't help listening to. It wasn't a normal honking, like geese. It was something more than that. It was birds talking, and that was the only time I'd ever heard that.

My dad smiled. It was light enough to see that. "Whistlers," he said. "Swans." He listened for a moment more then said, "They're about a mile up. Moving south."

Taking my gun from me, he leaned it against the wall. Then he picked me up and carried me out of the back of the blind very carefully, and squatted next to me so he was as tall as I was. He pointed straight up, and the canvas of his worn-out hunting jacket scraped my ear. I followed his arm up, past the out-stretched finger that he didn't even have a glove on, and then way, way past that. They were so high the sun was on them, when it wasn't even near to touching us. They were stretched out in Vs, long ones, but all lopsided, with one leg longer than the other. I remember wishing they could have gotten the Vs straighter. They were just tiny arrows of birds, and they were a mix of red and pink, the way the sun was hitting them. For a long time I thought they were always that color.

Then there was a rush of something through the air above our heads, close, and my dad jumped back into the blind, still holding me. The ducks were coming in.

He handed me my gun again, and I pointed it at the front wall of the blind, angling it up at the space he shot through. "When I say so," he said, "we'll stand up and you pick out a duck, whichever one is closest. Point the gun at him and follow him with it."

He straightened in his crouch so he could see over the wall, and then said, "Now."

I stood up and started to raise the gun. There were five ducks coming in, all with their wings making those upside-down Us. Sliding down and at us. But I didn't point the gun. My dad's went off and I'm sure a duck fell. He hardly ever misses. But I was staring at the front wall of the blind. He'd torn it down. I could see the damage, and I knew right away he'd done it so I would be able to see over it to shoot when I stood up. I looked at him just as he dropped another duck with his second barrel. That he'd actually torn down his blind for me surprised me more than anything he'd ever done in my life.

He looked at me with the look he always had after he shot and killed. Glazed, kind of, but happy and sad all at once. "Why didn't you shoot?" he asked, but I knew he wasn't done yet. He was still seeing those ducks coming in at him, though they were long gone by now.

I waited, then said, "My gun's empty."

He laughed and dug in a pocket of his vest and handed me two shells. Before he showed me how to load, he showed how I should hold the gun and how to look down the barrels without seeing anything but the bead on the very end. Then he loaded it and we sat down, and no more ducks came.

I opened my gun now and then, just to make sure the shells were still there. I kept wishing he would see the ducks and say, "Now," so I could stand up and shoot. I asked him once if he thought more ducks would come, and he laughed real low, like he does sometimes, but he didn't say anything.

We waited for a long time, and my dad started to talk, whispering the whole time, about jump shooting, and pit blinds, and different kind of decoy spreads, and how ducks would come in to them, and I listened just to hear his voice.

The blind was heating up, and it began to have that dark, swampy smell to it. Sometimes in school, all the way down in

California, that smell would come to me out of the blue, and I'd forget whatever we were supposed to be learning. I took a couple of deep breaths, but then my dad asked, "How's your mother getting along?"

I looked down at the mud. He'd never once mentioned her or asked about California since we'd moved away, and I would've died before bringing it up. Mom was always saying how lucky we were to live in California now, and I knew that wasn't something Dad would want to hear. I didn't say anything for a long time, but he kept waiting.

"She's married," I mumbled, only saying that because I was sure he must've already known. "To a rich guy," I added. "A doctor."

My dad's a farmer, and I'd heard him talk enough to know how he felt about rich guys, guys who didn't work and sweat. That's why I called the doc a rich guy, to let him know how I felt. But my dad just nodded, and his eyes switched around the edge of the blind opening, checking for flight.

A duck came in from behind us and landed hard, right in with the decoys, before my dad had a chance to do anything. I could see it swimming around with the wooden ducks, and I wondered what it thought about them. The two my dad had shot were still floating out there too. "Are you going to shoot it?" I asked. It was the longest time I'd ever watched a duck that wasn't out of range.

"It'll help bring in more," he said.

I watched that duck for a long time, thinking of how they looked flying, when my dad shot. I knew I didn't have the slightest chance of even touching one. I moved to the opening and poked my gun out. "I can shoot her," I said.

My dad took me by the shoulder and sat me down again. "You can't shoot them on the water," he said. "That's the worst thing you can do."

I sat on the bench and watched that duck swimming around out there, making ripples in with all the wooden ducks. In a little while my dad asked me how I liked my new dad. I told him I only had one dad, and he rubbed my shoulder.

"There were a lot of things your mother couldn't understand about me," he said, his hand still on my shoulder. "She's all right, though. But it was wrong for her to take you. At your age a boy needs his father more than his mother."

I glanced out of the blind, at the duck and the decoys, dark against the morning sheen of the water. The sky was opening, like I always pictured it when I was in California—big enough to hold anything. I could tell he was looking at me, but I didn't know what he wanted me to say. I just kept staring out at the sky and at the buttes, their edges and cuts beginning to show in the sunrise.

There was a whistle of wings overhead, and I could see my dad tense and forget what he had on his mind. But the ducks flew on and he relaxed. The top inch of black mud on the floor was melted now, and it stuck to my boots. I lifted my boots up one at a time, listening to the sucking sounds. In the summer it'd pull your boots right off. I almost smiled.

"I've been talking to your mom," he said.

I didn't look at him. I held my shotgun and put both my feet flat on the ground and thought of the torn-down blind and of him asking me how Mom was when he'd been talking to her all along.

"I told her about a boy being with his father once he gets to be your age. I told her how important I thought it was. I told her I thought you'd like it better up here."

It was hot all of a sudden and I took my mittens off, and I was surprised to feel how cold the gun was. I held my hands on it to make them cold and to make me think of anything other than what he was talking about. But it didn't work. I'd known they'd never stopped fighting—Mom was always talking about that, too. Just before I'd come up she'd told me the doctor wanted to adopt me. She hadn't told me that my dad wanted me too.

"She didn't say it in so many words really," he kept going. "But we agreed to ask you first, before we got into any of it with the lawyers."

I heard wings coming in, and for the first time ever my dad wasn't moving to them. I looked up to see if he heard them, and he was just looking down at me. I could practically feel my arms and legs coming out of their sockets, with Mom pulling on one end and Dad on the other.

I jumped up before I knew what I was doing, and I saw how hopeless the ducks in the air were, and I pointed my gun at the one on the water. Her neck was stretched up, calling to the others at the very second I shot. There was spray all around her, I think, but I couldn't really tell because the shotgun knocked me back and made my eyes all watery.

I nearly dropped the gun, but my dad grabbed it, and me, hard. "What the hell was that all about?" he said, whispering with his teeth together so it sounded mad enough to be shouting. "Didn't I just tell you that you never shoot . . ."

I was watching my dad, trying to figure out how I could tell him anything, but when he trailed off like that right in the middle of chewing me out, I couldn't think of anything anymore. I was scared and I wished I'd shot at the ones in the air, but I hadn't. I watched his eyes, but they were a bad thing to see. I looked at the floor, then, and I almost thought I could see that mud smell coming right out of the ground, like heat wrinkling off a parking lot.

"I see," he said. Then he said it again, "I see." I could tell his teeth weren't together anymore, and he didn't sound mad. He sounded like a way I'd never heard him. I looked up, and his face was all soft and his mouth kind of quivered like he was trying to say something besides "I see" but couldn't quite figure out what it might be.

I looked out of the broken blind, just to keep from looking at his face, and I saw that I had hit that duck. It was upside down now, one orange leg making slow kicks in the air. It looked completely different than it had when it was calling to the ducks that had flown away when I shot.

I said, "No. You don't see at all," and when he asked me what I meant, I could only say, "I don't know."

My dad said, "Let's go then. There won't be anything else here."

He stood up and waited a second at the door of the blind. I didn't move, though, and I listened to him hesitate then walk away, crackling through the dead and frozen reeds that surrounded the blind.

It was bright inside the blind by then, and I looked at the gun in my lap, at the swirl the grain made in the stock and at that name again. It was the same name that was on my dad's gun. I'd checked.

I thought of my dad out here by himself in the cold, tearing down the front of his blind just so it would be ready for me when I came. And I thought of him up in his house, polishing and polishing this gun until it was so perfect. I wondered what else he did up here, all by himself. I'd never wondered that before, and I couldn't think of anything. It made Montana seem smaller than it ever had.

I stood up then, unloading my gun, like Dad had. I smelled the open barrels, but they smelled like burnt powder now, not like my dad's hands.

I ran out of the blind, to catch up to him, but he was standing right at the edge of the reeds, staring out at the dead ducks and the decoys and the ice. His face was still slack, like everything'd been pulled out of it, and I suddenly knew that was how my mom's face was going to look when she found out what they'd made me decide. But she had the doctor and my dad didn't have anything but this emptiness. That was the only thing he had, that and this gun, and he'd just given it all to me.

I crackled through the reeds too, and when I was next to him I said I would stay with him and that I was sorry I'd shot that duck. My voice, in the cold, empty air, was louder than I would have guessed.

My dad looked down at me and put his hand on my shoulder. "I'm sorry I couldn't've made your mom stay too."

I was hoping his face would light up again, like it had when he'd pointed up at the swans, but then I saw it wasn't something like that. It would be dark again, and we would be back in the house, cleaning our guns and putting them into his cabinet, before I'd think his face might someday look that way again.

Trumpeter

THEY LEFT THE BLACK RING in the snow as soon as they guessed it was light enough to shoot. They were close to the creek, and they had not rebuilt the fire this morning and hadn't talked in anything above a whisper since they'd crawled from their sleeping bags. Since this was their last trip, they had left their tent at home and slept beneath the huge, low branches of the spruce, as they had in the beginning, before they could afford tents.

They griped quietly as they pulled on the frozen chest waders, shaking their heads and smiling. There were three goose carcasses and a pile of ducks, all frozen and stacked beside their snowshoes. They were close enough to the creek that they would not need the snowshoes for the first jump. When they heard the quackings, they looked at each other and smiled. They were practically on top of the ducks, and once they were dressed they stopped complaining about the cold.

The thigh-deep snow was like quicksand but it muffled the stiff squeaks of the cold rubber waders. They moved through the black tree trunks and the dark, bluish green of the spruce that grew all the way to the ground, and their breath smoked into the clear, gray air. Walt looked to the sky and thought it would be no problem shooting at anything up against it. Ahead, in the woods, the lighting was chancier.

It surprised him how much his move had already changed things, when he had yet to drive a mile away from here. Lyle was breaking the trail, as he had all day yesterday. It was something they'd taken turns at before. Lyle, probably without realizing it, was already treating him like a guest.

Walt hurried two steps to say he would lead, but they were already at the edge of the trees. They could hear ducks everywhere, and they started to point, showing how they would split, trapping the ducks between them. But then they heard one honk, and things were suddenly more important. They knelt down together and talked into one another's ears.

Lyle thought the honk was from the bend they had been stalking. Walt thought it had come from a little farther downstream. They couldn't agree, and Walt finally said he would take the downstream leg of their pincer and he would stretch it farther downstream than usual, hoping to snare the geese too.

Walt smiled at the mist of his breath frozen on the fur of Lyle's hat, and they separated. It was all crawling from here, and though the snow made almost everything more difficult, it made the sneak on the ducks murderously easy. With their guns tucked backward they plowed trails for themselves below the level of the snow, hidden from everything that wasn't directly above them.

There was a ripple of the odd feeding murmurs of geese, and Walt knew he had it right. He pushed the front of his waders against his chest so they wouldn't scoop in snow, and he crawled forward on one elbow. It was hard moving and his lungs didn't have the right kind of room to work, and though he rested, Walt was breathing hard by the time he was close to the creek.

He lifted his head above the snow, knowing he shouldn't but unable to stop himself. The creek was open only because it was fed by hot springs, and with the frigid morning, the fog above the water was as thick as a smoke screen. The water was the same flat, silver-gray as the fog, and the darker shapes of the ducks and geese seemed suspended in the murky air.

Walt dropped back beneath the snow. This was murderous. He wasn't ten yards from the creek, but the steam was so heavy he could have gotten this close without the cover of the snow.

As he waited for the light, Walt wondered if it would help. If the fog turned brilliant, it would be almost impossible to see at all. But maybe a wind would come up, moving the mist off the creek long enough to make the jump. He and Lyle had made this kind of jump for years, and they'd had to wait for the light and the fog both, but his heart hadn't slowed since he'd heard the geese and seen the creek covered with the foggy silhouettes. He doubted that would ever fail him, no matter how far away he had to move from here.

Walt sat back in the snow with his feet under him, ready to stand and fire. He took off his heavy mittens and slipped two more shells between the fingers of his left hand. With Lyle pressing in from the other end of the creek's loop, the birds often were confused enough to give them more than the first two shots.

He wiped the snow off the barrels of his shotgun and listened to the birds on the water. He could pick out ducks and geese, and once he heard another voice he could not place.

With one hand over the breach to muffle the sound, he opened the barrels and removed the shells. He checked to make sure no snow had clogged the barrels, and as he replaced the shells he heard the birds erupt. He tensed at the first flat slaps of heavy wings against water, and then nothing was distinguishable in the cacophony of honking and quacking and splashing water and the hum of the stiff, cold air through the thousands of feathers.

Walt jumped up as he snapped shut the barrels of his gun.

Everything that had been on the water in front of him was now in the air, filling the fog with streaming, fleeting, filmy shadows. Walt swung on the largest shape he could make out. There were two quick shots from upstream that Walt wouldn't realize he had heard until after the firing was over. And then Walt fired, even as he became aware that the shape he was following was not quite right. A leg dropped, and the shape began to falter as it disappeared in the grayness. Walt swung on another, a duck this time, and it collapsed and another shot came from upstream.

Walt did not look away from the fog bank of flying shapes as he dropped in his second two shells. He closed his shotgun, already bringing it to his shoulder when the enormous white bird broke from the fog and came over him, the wind rushing in claps beneath its wings. Walt ducked, and he recognized the first shape that had not been right and he lowered his gun, the whistling beats of those wings still over his head.

It was suddenly quiet, and Walt realized how deafening the noise over the creek had been. Then Lyle whooped from upstream and Walt could hear him splashing in the creek. He walked through the last ten yards of snow and stepped into the steaming water, watching it melt the snow from his waders as he waited for Lyle's goose to drift to him. He put his mittens back on and picked the goose up behind its head. It was heavy. Walt set it back in the water, blocking its drift with his legs, and Lyle became visible in the fog, pushing his way downstream through the water, holding two more geese.

"Well?" Lyle cried. He held the two geese out at arm's length. Walt picked up the one he had stopped and said, "This is yours too."

"I knew he dropped!" Lyle shouted. "I lost him in the fog. It's spooky in here, isn't it?"

Lyle had nearly reached Walt, and Walt looked at the geese he held. The black neck feathers were matted and rumpled where Lyle had grabbed them; otherwise they looked as perfect as they always did.

"What'd you get? You only shot twice?"

Lyle took the goose Walt had and said, "You spooked this one. He came right at me out of the fog." Despite his excitement he was whispering again in the muting fog. Then he looked at Walt and asked again, "What did you get?"

"I knocked down a duck. He's on the shore over here someplace." Walt had turned away from Lyle and was pushing through the slow flow of warm water and heavy weeds to the snowy bank of shore.

Lyle followed him and threw his geese into the crater in the snow where Walt had waited to shoot. Walt was already casting around in the willows that stuck only a few feet from the snow and Lyle asked where he thought it had gone down.

Just then Walt leaned forward. There was a hole in the snow, and he stuck his hand into it and pulled out a mallard drake. The snow stuck to it, and it did not look nearly as neat as the geese, which had fallen into the water.

"Nice greenhead," Lyle said, and he smiled. "Nice, small, single greenhead."

Walt looked up and smiled back. If it wasn't for that white bird flying over him, he would have laughed and everything would have been fine. They would walk back to camp and make a fire and coffee, and they would talk of the jump, and Lyle would tell him how the three geese had come down, big as airplanes. Then they would put their snowshoes on and follow the creek to the Snake and hike it. They would jump the holes they knew there, where the hunting was harder and there was no way of knowing if there were birds in the holes or not without stalking them as carefully as if you knew there would be birds. They would jump the creek once more at dusk, then hike back to his truck and drive into town. The next morning he and Lyle would shake hands and their wives would hug, and then he would start the long drive to San Diego where there wasn't any snow and trumpeter swans did not appear out of fog banks and fly ten feet over your head.

Walt had wondered about ignoring that first shape he had fired at, but he said, "I hit something else, Lyle. Hard, but it didn't drop. Let's get the snowshoes and start looking. It could have made the river."

Lyle was already turned back to camp, slogging down the trail Walt had crushed into the snow. "Goose?" he asked.

"I'm not sure," Walt said. The way he spoke made Lyle turn around. "I thought so until I shot. But there was something wrong. I dropped a leg, I saw that." Walt tried to walk around Lyle, but Lyle started again and Walt followed him back to camp.

"A swan came out of the fog right afterward," he said, more to himself than to Lyle. "He came right at me. I heard them out there just before you jumped everything. I just couldn't place the sound. It was all that fog. It's like having cataracts."

Lyle didn't say anything until they reached the camp. They sat on the logs they had cleared the snow from and tied on their snowshoes. "Are you sure you hit it?" he asked.

"Positive. I was practically on top of them."

"Are you sure it was a trumpeter?"

"I don't know. At the last second it didn't look like a goose. But it was in the fog. It seemed smaller than a trumpeter. Smaller than the one that broke out of the fog." Walt stood up and tested the fit of his snowshoes.

"Let's go see," Lyle said, trying to sound cheerful. "We'll probably just find the world's biggest goose."

Walt shook his head and started to walk back to where he had sat waiting to shoot. It was the first time he'd led all trip.

They searched through the willows but found no holes in the snow or any sign of a crash landing. They didn't turn around until they came to the Snake. The big river moved past in several channels, heavy and black, bordered by snow. They split up and moved back to the creek where Walt had shot.

"Maybe you just winged it," Lyle said. Even with the snow-shoes the going wasn't simple, and they were both sending big clouds of breath into the air. It was lighter now, and the fog over the creek was easier to see through.

"Let's check the creek," Walt said. "I know I saw a leg go down." He took his snowshoes off and stepped into the water, and Lyle hugged the bank. The snow was undisturbed on the banks. It curved out over the water and then tucked into the shore like a pillow. Anything trying to hide or escape would have left a mark.

Something with wings burst from the edge of the creek, and Walt and Lyle both started to bring their guns up. Then they both called, "Snipe," at the same time. Walt let out his breath slowly, and Lyle smiled back at him and shrugged, lowering his gun.

Walt waded to the confluence with the Snake. Lyle took his gun while he pawed his way out of the water and up onto the bank. "It's anybody's guess now," Lyle said. "What do you want to do?"

"Let's check a little more." Walt looked up and down the wide, open valley of the river. "Let's cross over to the middle and kick around some. All right? I know I hit it hard."

Even as he said that Walt was beginning to feel safer about it. Whatever the bird was, it had made it at least the few hundred yards to the river. If they made it that far they usually escaped completely. He doubted that they often survived, but they became one of the birds that you looked for as hard as you could and you could stop thinking about eventually. He knew if he had proof he had killed a trumpeter, it would not be something he could give up and forget.

He began to wonder if a leg really had dropped. He was beginning to doubt every detail of those foggy few seconds, and without proof he wouldn't know what had happened or what had been merely impressions.

They moved downstream to the first crossing and slid down the beaver slide into the shallow water. The Snake was colder than the creek, and it pressed their waders around their legs until they reached the shallows on the far side of the channel. Lyle put his snowshoes back on and headed into the island, while Walt stayed in the shallow water, moving upstream until he was across from the creek exit.

Walt stopped at the broken snow on the bank there and wondered how they hadn't seen it from the opposite shore. "Over here," he called. In the cold, clear air over the river his voice was stronger than he expected.

Walt stepped out of the river, and Lyle was with him in a few seconds. They looked at the snow without speaking. Something had crashed into the very top edge of the bank, nearly clearing it. There was a large dish where the chest hit and a sharp line from a wing edge. More dents and scrapes followed in the light snow, where the bird had flipped over. Finally, a few yards farther on, were the running footprints, only a few of them. The bird must still have had some momentum. The scrapes of the wing-tip feathers carried on beyond the footprints and then disappeared. There was one fleck of blood, like a bright match head, in the first divot of the breast.

"Doesn't look hit that hard," Lyle said, and when Walt didn't say anything, he added, "Looks like he's using both legs, anyway."

Walt bent down to look and wasn't sure. The right footprint seemed weak and pigeon-toed. "Look at the wingspan," he said.

Lyle bent down too, pretending it was something that needed studying. "Be a damn big goose."

"It isn't a goose," Walt said, and they didn't say anything more. Walt started to follow the direction the footprints pointed in, and Lyle fell in behind him.

They snowshoed across the flat, buried gravel bar and dipped down into an old channel. Some snags poked through the snow on both sides of the depression, stark gray against the smooth, white snow. Before they were halfway across the bottom, Walt saw the scars of the second impact next to the huge root system of a mostly buried snag. The bird had dipped into the channel and been unable to climb back out.

By the time he reached the cratered snow, Walt had already seen the swan. It had flopped from the impact site to the protection of the rosette of gnarled roots. The swan had backed into the roots, then, and spread its wings out, ready to fight, but had died before anything challenged it. Its head was draped over its back, at the end of that long neck, almost as if it was asleep. There was only the slightest flecking of blood on the gray of its breast. It was not a sheer white adult but a smaller, grayer cygnet. Lyle whispered, "Damn."

Walt leaned his shotgun against the roots and picked up the bird by its neck. He tipped to the side with the weight and was not able to lift it entirely off the ground because of the length of the neck. He laid it down again, stretched out on its back.

There were shades of brown through the gray, and there was a band on the bird's broken leg. Walt squatted beside the swan and read the numbers out loud, for no reason that he could've explained. A BB had hit the leg just at the end of the feathers, so the muscles still worked but the leg simply flopped at the end of them. Walt remembered the weak print of the right foot and let go of the broken leg.

"I don't feel much like hunting, Lyle."

"It's dead, Walt. It could have died from a hundred other things. There's nothing we can do now."

"It didn't die of a hundred other things, though." Walt picked up his gun, to have something to hold. There were two round river rocks held up in the air by the grip of the tree roots, and Walt brushed the snow off them.

"Let's keep going," Lyle said. "Just like we planned. The girls don't expect us until tonight. Breakfast will work wonders."

"How many trumpeters are there?" Walt asked. He picked up the cygnet again, by the neck, and started dragging it back the way they had come. Its body left a ditch in the snow, with periodic slashes to the side from a flopping wing.

"They're on the comeback, Walt." Lyle started to follow him. "This isn't going to wipe them out." The wing made a flapping noise every time it dug into the snow.

"What are you going to do with it?" Lyle asked.

"Take it to Game and Fish, I guess."

Lyle didn't say anything to that. Walt put down the bird and they both took off their snowshoes and waded across the Snake again. The swan dragged in the water and then through the snow on the other bank, and the water and snow mixed and froze on the feathers.

They stopped and picked up the duck, which fit in Walt's vest, and Lyle threw a pair of geese over his shoulder and carried the third in his gun hand.

When they reached camp, Lyle dropped the geese in with the others, but Walt stretched the swan out by itself and looked at it while Lyle started the fire. They'd had everything ready to go before they'd left, and the flames crept over the tinder and took hold in the bigger sticks.

Looking at the dusty gray young swan, stretched out in the snow and dead, Walt felt sweaty and sick, and he struggled out of his chest waders and threw them over the carcass. He changed quickly into his wool pants and heavy packs, but having the bird hidden did not make him feel any less embarrassed or guilty.

"Not much of an end, is it?" Walt asked.

"It's all right. It's not like you'll never be back up here again."

"Sometimes that's the way it feels, though."

Walt remembered the waiting, with his heart going too fast, and he remembered the wild second of wings and fog and shapes and shooting. With the proof of the cygnet, everything was hard and clear in his mind. He remembered how outrageously loud the birds had been, and he could hear when Lyle shot and could remember that he had not hesitated until after he had pulled the trigger himself. He could remember the mallard, stopped short and crumpling, but he did not think of that.

The adult had come out of the fog as if it had been a part of it. The huge, swooping wings had lunged at the air, and the neck had been stretched so far that Walt wondered what it was striving toward. He looked to where the young cygnet was hidden under his waders, but he could still see the tangled feathers with the ice and the snow crusted into them, and he whispered that he was sorry.

Lyle told him not to worry about it, they'd have plenty more hunts.

Walt looked at him and said, "That's not what I meant, but I'm sorry about that too."

Lyle was intent on the fire and the coffee. He nudged coals and burning sticks around the blackened pot and said, "You don't have to take that swan in."

"Yes I do. I know it won't make any difference. I'll pay the fine." Walt touched his waders with his toe. "I don't imagine they get one to study very often."

"You know," Lyle said, "You've shot hundreds of ducks and geese and so have I. We've tried to build this trip into something just because you've been transferred." Lyle lifted the top off the pot, though nothing could have boiled that fast. "But even with all the buildup, all this trip is is shooting more ducks and geese.

I'll remember the triple I got on geese. But I've done that before. So have you. We've both jumped this thing when the fog's been this spooky."

Walt didn't say anything, and Lyle added, "It kind of fits, really. It's kind of the way we would've remembered this trip anyway."

Then Lyle shrugged and said, "It happens. I never told you about the sow I killed before I saw the cubs." Lyle fiddled with the pot. "It goes away eventually, but it's never something you forget."

Walt watched Lyle squatted before the fire, the smoke stinging his eyes and the frost of his breath caught on his mustache and collar. He didn't believe Lyle had ever shot a bear that way.

When they broke camp they realized they would have to make two trips to bring out all the birds. It was nearly a mile to the truck, and although there were only two ducks and the swan left, Lyle walked back with Walt.

They kicked out the last of the fire and buried it with snow. Without the guns, Walt was able to carry the swan over his shoulder and keep it from dragging on the ground. He bent forward, a little with the weight and a little to make sure it didn't drag. Lyle carried a duck in each hand, swinging them as he walked, and he began to talk of how it would be next year, when Walt would be just one more lousy Californian coming up for a week of shooting.

Walt wasn't really listening, but he tried to smile. He felt the weight of the swan on his back, and he looked at the head, which was close to his own face now the way he was carrying it. The beak was black at both ends but immature and pink in the middle, and the eye he could see was open and black. He wondered if the wardens would let him keep it.

Megadethed

WHEN MY SON MARK WALKED into my den and said, "I suppose that turkey hunt could be sort of fun," I looked up quickly from my work, but he turned and walked out before I had a chance to catch more than a glimpse of his ever-present Walkman and his sleeveless black Megadeth T-shirt. I'd asked if he wanted to come along more from a sense of duty than any belief he might really be interested. About a year ago he'd run smack into an adolescence just like mine, when everything my parents did, if not obviously calculated to annoy me or deprive me of my rights, seemed the dumbest possible thing in the world.

I picked my pen back up and couldn't help but smile. Maybe there really was a light at the end of his tunnel.

The following weekend he said he needed to practice so he "wouldn't look like a complete wimp." I took him up to the gravel pit with the pump twenty I'd bought for him when he turned twelve. It hadn't been fired in a couple of years.

Mark fired his first shot into an abandoned washing machine, from the hip. He squinted grimly as if he'd just barely won a shootout, and I chewed him out. I got a black scowl in return but I kept after him. "No playing around with this, Mark. You know better than that."

"Like I'm going to kill you or something," he answered, trying hard to look wronged.

He settled down some when I started to throw the pigeons, but he hit about one in three and I could see him begin to simmer. I gave little bits of advice until he finally said, "Hey, you want to try?"

He knew I could shoot and I felt bad for him, remembering how the anger and frustration could build until you said things you knew didn't make sense even as you said them.

I knocked off ten, missing one, though he was throwing them as trickily as he could. He threw so hard two disintegrated as they left the thrower. "You're going to hurt your arm," I said.

"Trade," he muttered, holding the thrower out to me, not looking me in the eye.

We went out again on Sunday, and then he asked to go again Monday evening. I asked if his shoulder wasn't sore and he said, "Give me a break."

He improved quickly, growing less surly with each shattered clay, and he began to ask what the other guys shot like. When he was twelve and the gun was new he'd startled me with his ability. I'd given him a membership in the skeet club for his fourteenth, but adolescence laid him low after only a round or two. I told him the other guys, my hunting partners, were both aces, which was stretching it, but I couldn't help myself.

We developed a routine, going out every evening before dinner, making the most of the short spring days. Shooting was the first thing we'd done together in a couple of years, and when I complained that he couldn't hear me call "Pull," which wasn't quite true, he even began leaving his Walkman at home.

Over the weeks Mark started to bring his own extra shells

and even pigeons, the new lime green kind, and we'd stay later and later. He said the fluorescent birds were easier to see in the dusk, and who knows, we might not see the turkeys till dark and we might as well prepare for everything. In turn I bought a ground-mounted pigeon thrower and started to throw two at a time. Pretty soon I began to count on seeing the black, dusty burst of a direct hit not once but twice. I told him he worked the pump so fast it sounded like an auto. He shrugged, and though I could see him try not to, he smiled. We pressed each other to see who'd break more.

Finally, though I'd grown less and less impatient for it, the weekend of the hunt arrived, and Les and Carl came over to load up the trailer. Mark hung around the edges, the only boy, but he made a real effort to be helpful. It was so nice to see his ears without the plugs of the Walkman's black sponges.

The next morning Carl and Les drove out together, leaving me the long drive alone with Mark. I kissed Teresa good-bye, and from the darkness she whispered, "Nervous?"

I was surprised to discover that's exactly how I felt, and I denied it twice before I reached the bedroom door.

We stopped at the Mini-Mart for coffee and donuts, and Mark surprised me again, filling up an extra-large cup for himself. Once back on the road I said, "I didn't know you drank coffee."

He answered through his donut. "Most mornings Caleb and I stop at the Daily Grind before going to school."

I peered down the headlights' path and thought of the questions Teresa and I had asked each other about his early departures, about drugs, about all manner of evil. "Why don't you drink it at home?"

"Didn't know if you guys'd let me," he answered, taking a noisy slurp through the plastic lid of the Styrofoam cup. He hadn't yet learned the secret of that, and after a few more tries he pulled the lid off, saying, "What a stupid thing." If he spilled any on himself later, he didn't let me know.

The rest of the way out he kept up most of the talk, asking more questions about Carl and Les, about turkeys, about how to tell the males from the females. I got in a few of my own, about Caleb, his lifelong friend who seemed to undergo the same changes at the same instant as Mark, about the band they were trying to get started, but he was pretty close about it. "Still can't find a drummer" was all he offered.

I wanted to answer that with, "Maybe there is a God after all." At one time Mark had been an unstoppable teaser, able to take as well as he gave, but now there was no telling how he'd take anything and I didn't risk pushing.

When we reached the campground, Carl and Les were just getting out of their truck. Everybody worked setting up camp, and once we had a little fire started in the stove, Carl and Les stretched out their cots and lay down for the pre-evening nap. Mark looked at me, and I knew he didn't want to just go to sleep after driving all this way. Though I thought the cots looked awful nice, I asked if he wanted to take a quick walk, get the lay of the land, and we were off.

I steered clear of the roost area we always hunted, and we strolled through the open ponderosa woods. We kept quiet, but walking around like that was pretty useless as far as getting any turkeys went, and I took the time to explain more about turkeys and their habits. "Remember to aim at the head. That's the hardest thing," I said. "Those bodies look so huge and easy it's pretty hard not to throw away a shot or two at them. They can seem damn near armored."

He kept nodding, and I knew that after a month of practice he considered himself a marksman. Head shots would be no problem.

We were still ambling along like that, whispering, Mark just starting to say how nice the woods smelled, with the sun working on the downed needles and all, when we crested a tiny little rise. The two-foot-long stem of grass I'd been chewing on fell out of my mouth, for standing right in front of us, not thirty yards off, were two huge toms, apparently as astonished as us.

One of the toms launched straight up through the trees, but the other hesitated, and Mark's gun went off right beside me and I saw the slow turkey bowl over, feathers flying. Before I could say anything, Mark hooted, "All right!" and charged toward the turkey he'd knocked over, his gun dangling at his side.

I'm sure Mark was still picturing that impressive blast of feathers, and there was a moment when I think he didn't even see the turkey get up. There was nothing I could do with Mark between the bird and me except shout, "Mark!" and watch the big, old tom do a Jesse Owens straight through the thick brush while Mark tried to skid to a stop, raise his gun, aim, and fire all at the same time. I could see the barrel jerk as he pulled the trigger, so wired on adrenaline it took a second before he realized he hadn't pumped in a new shell.

He kicked at the ground and let out a rip of swearing I hadn't heard from him before. I came up beside him and whispered, "Those body shots are awful hard not to take."

"I blew the hell out of him," he complained, breathing hard.

"Probably," I answered. "You just didn't blow the life out of him too."

"Well, shit! Now what?"

"First off, remember your mouth. You sound like a sailor."

He rolled his eyes, but he looked genuinely surprised. Shit was one of the softer words he'd used.

"Now we start looking for him," I said, and I had that bad taste in my mouth, the one I get every time I hit something and have to start a search I doubt will meet with success.

"He'll just fly away, won't he?"

"Could. Maybe you broke a wing." But I'd seen him run, wings tight to his body, nothing dragging, nothing looking damaged at all.

We stepped forward to where the turkeys had been and saw their big-footed scratch marks in the dusty-dry dirt. "Look at all the feathers," Mark said.

I picked some up, broken wing feathers mostly, a few chest, no skin or blood. "Sometimes they can be just like geese," I said. "Feathers like a bulletproof vest." When he was little Mark used to love helping me pluck geese. Occasionally a BB would drop out of the down and bounce across the floor. He kept the BBs he found in a little jar.

"How the hell are we going to find him?"

I said, "Watch the mouth," again, not bothering to look up at his expression. "We'll sit tight a little bit. See if he sickens up. You might have got a lucky one into his lungs. Then we'll try to follow him."

"Follow him?" Mark asked. "Through this?" He lifted his gun at the dry brush and grass.

I did look up at him then. "You pulled the trigger," I said. "Got any better ideas?"

He sat down in the dirt and toyed with a broken wing feather. "You'd think that'd kill anything," he said quietly.

"Another day it might. But they're tough, old birds."

We sat and waited for about twenty minutes before starting out on the trail, which we were able to follow, mostly by broken feathers stuck on the brush, for all of thirty feet. Then the brush and the feathers gave way to a featureless mat of last year's grass, green sprouts just starting to poke through.

We began circling, our expectations fading with each round farther from the point of the shooting. Finally we were just ambling, always farther away from any sort of hope. But Mark didn't give up, or even mention it. Once he asked if we should try calling, but I told him a wounded bird probably wouldn't be very interested in hens.

As dusk approached I admitted that if I had been alone, I wouldn't have kept at it this long, but Mark didn't answer. Finally I said, "That's it, Mark. We gave it our best shot. We've got to get back to the truck before it's dark."

We turned around, and on the trudge back Mark asked what would happen to the tom.

"Well he sure doesn't seem very hard hit, does he?" I said, trying to cheer him up. "I mean, he was able to put on a few miles, anyway."

"He sure looked hard hit when he flew over backwards."

"You can never tell by that. Could be a BB never got through his hide."

"What if some did?"

I plucked another piece of grass to chew. "If it buried in his chest muscle, he could heal up. I've found birds with encysted BBs in them."

"What if it got into his insides?"

I glanced over at Mark in the evening light, at his too-long hair, thinking of his fondness for a band called Megadeth. "Then he probably won't make it," I told him. "The wound could be mortal itself or it could infect."

"So it could take a long time?"

I kept watching Mark, saw the care with which he studied the ground, placed his steps. Somehow I was glad he was going through this, glad he was able to. "Probably not," I said. "Coyotes. Eagles. They usually don't let anything like that take too long."

Mark nodded as he continued to set his feet down so precisely one after the other. By the time we reached the truck, it was just about dark, and we unloaded our guns and drove back to camp without talking much.

The tent shone bright in the dark woods, the lantern inside already lit. "Looks like we're the last ones back," I said. "If they bothered going out at all."

Mark tried to give a little smile, and I threw aside the flap and stepped into the heat.

"How many'd you get?" Carl asked right away, turning from the stove holding a spatula and smiling at Mark. "Save any for the old men?"

"We found two big ones," Mark said, surprising me. "I knocked one over, but it ran and we couldn't find it."

Carl shook his head and said, "That's tough," but Les laughed and said, "So, you got the head-shot speech from the old man, did you? Well never mind all that crap. Just keep shooting till they're so full of lead they can't get up anymore. That's how you get turkeys."

Even Mark chuckled at that, and I said, "That's exactly how Les gets his. Sometimes he can even salvage a drumstick."

Les sputtered, pushing himself up from his cot and walking outside. When I looked at Carl he nodded, holding his hands out, not so far apart.

Then Les was back inside, dragging a little tom with him. "Check this out, Ace," he said to me, holding up the naked head so I could see the black hole in the back of it.

Carl said, "Shot it out of a tree in the last half second of shooting light."

"Out of a tree?" I asked, settling onto my cot.

"Don't tell me that's against your rules?" Les said.

"Out of a tree?" I asked again, rubbing my chin. "I'm not so sure about that."

"You shoot them on the ground, don't you?" Mark asked, and Les said, "God, I like that kid."

"Should've seen it," Carl said. "We were almost back to the

truck when that thing fluttered over us and landed in the tree. Scared us half to death."

"Shot in self-defense," Les admitted, and as they laughed they went over every detail of the hunt, and then went over it again. Mark asked a few questions but mostly sat and listened, and I wondered what he was thinking about, what he'd have to say to his gang about this back home. Was it something they'd laugh over—old coots telling stories about dead birds out in the woods? I wondered if he was close enough to Caleb to try to describe what had gone on inside him as we'd circled and circled, trying to kick up the bird he'd wounded, or even to describe what had caused him to shout and run in when he thought he'd killed it cleanly.

For an instant I pictured them taking a break from their practice in Caleb's garage, the din of the guitars still ringing in their ears, who knows, maybe a haze of pot smoke clouding the air, and Mark saying, "Should've seen them, running around like killing some stupid bird's the most important thing in the world."

But that was pure imagination—I didn't know how he thought—and in the sleeping bag that night, with Carl and Les starting to snore, I wondered what Mark might consider the most important thing in the world.

The next morning we were up before dawn, throwing down a quick cup of coffee and a roll before heading to the roost trees. Carl and Les and I had hunted here so long we no longer bothered to scout it preseason. The roost had produced for years.

Once out of the trucks we hesitated only long enough to let Mark in on the strategies we'd followed all those years. "I'm the driver," I told him. "Carl and Les set up on each side of the draw you'll see in a minute. I get into the roost area, and when they come out I take the best and push the little ones to them."

"My ass," Les said. "You're old man's just too ornery to hunt with anyone else."

"Loner Paul," Carl called me.

"Don't listen to anything they say," I told Mark. "Today you're hunting with me. Those two'll be lucky to even see a turkey."

Mark smiled but didn't say anything and we held each other's guns as we took turns slipping through the fence in the murky light. We circled along the edge of the last field, the winter wheat already up and green, and just before entering the trees Mark asked, "Do you really go alone every year?"

"Just this part."

"I do that too," Mark whispered "Go around just by myself. I kind of like it."

We crept along in the woods then, the ground soft and quiet if we watched where we stepped. When we were near where the draw dropped into the roost, I said, "Let's take five here. The roost is just ahead. We'll wait for them to come down."

The trees were thicker here, darker, but still open enough to peer through, searching against the gray sky for the black, oblong shapes of roosted turkeys. We sat in the duff and long ponderosa needles, craning our necks up at the web of branches. "We should be able to hear them gabbling anytime now," I whispered, leaning toward Mark's ear.

He nodded and we sat tight. When the gobble blurted through the draw, I saw him sit straighter, and I leaned over again. "That's Les," I whispered. "Hear how he wavers on the end?"

Mark shrugged, his all-purpose gesture, and I figured he was probably seeing that turkey of his again, feathers flying, wondering if he'd get another chance.

Les gobbled again a few minutes later, and this time it

seemed to wake up the birds in the roost. They began with a few quiet murmurs and then started talking back and forth in earnest. Mark whispered, "Sounds like ducks."

It didn't really sound anything like ducks, but I knew what he meant, something feeding-murmurish about it, and I was about to say that when I heard the first wing beats. I grinned. "They're down," I said. "Remember the head."

I touched his elbow and we stood up together. I pointed, indicating that we should spread out, and we took our first cautious steps forward.

I grimaced at every dry crackle beneath my feet, and I glanced over at Mark. He was doing everything right, looking around after every step, even searching the branches above him. He turned my way once, his face set deadly serious, and I was just able to hold back my smile until he turned away.

None of the brush had really started leafing out past buds, and it wasn't hard to see through to the ground. I studied everything I could, step after step, and was beginning to edge around a big old, ponderosa when I caught Mark motioning for me to stop. I froze, then slowly stretched to get a glimpse of what he could be looking at.

I couldn't make out anything and I turned for help. Mark was pointing his gun into the trees, nearly straight up. I glanced that way, and the blast of his shot shook into the trees, tearing through the branches.

Suddenly there were turkeys everywhere, launching from the trees I thought they'd already left. Mark fired again, before the echo of his first shot had even started and I saw something tumbling through the branches of his tree. He fired again, green-needled twigs cascading down around his shots.

Just above the ground the branches of Mark's tree thinned, and I saw the falling turkey flapping wildly out of control, a sure head shot, and I whooped, forgetting to even make a try at any of the other birds. Before the turkey had cleared the opening, Mark fired a fourth time, and I watched the feathers fly.

"You got him already!" I shouted.

The woods were quiet for a moment and I watched Mark, the pump already worked, his gun tight to his shoulder, aiming over the fifteen yards that separated him from the very still body of the turkey on the ground. "I think you got this one," I said again, not completely successful in stifling my laugh. "I think you pâtéd him."

A single shot rang out in the distance and I said, "Carl," and Mark finally lowered his gun.

He stepped carefully, holding his gun at the ready, and I really did start to laugh. After he stooped down and picked the turkey up by the neck, a truly long, fat-bottomed bird, I said, "Are you sure he's dead?"

Mark laughed then too, a wonderful sound in the still woods, and he moved up the hill toward me. "Take a look at him," he said, and he started to run, the big tom not slowing him down at all. "Take a look at him!" he shouted, hoisting the bird up at arm's length.

He was a gorgeous bird, all iridescent sheens where the feathers hadn't been disheveled by shot, and I said so.

"I think my first shot got him in the head. Man, even way up there I could see his beard! Look at him!"

I let his excited babble wear itself out before I said, "No doubt that was a display of shooting. You better tag him."

"Oh man, I would've forgot that completely," he said, laughing, digging through his pockets for the tag. I took the chance to feel the bird, the broken neck and wings and legs. Then Mark tugged him away from me to gut him, feeling the looseness himself.

"Think I hit him enough?" he asked, and he laughed out loud at himself, not sounding at all like a rock star.

I sat down beside him, plucking a stem of grass to chew on, and said, "You Megadethed his ass for sure."

Mark stopped his gutting and stared at me. "Megadethed?" he asked, then blurted, "Megadethed! Man, I don't believe it!" He laughed wildly. "Wait'll Caleb hears that!"

Mark saw Carl and Les first, coming up the hill toward us, Carl with a turkey slung over his shoulder. He looked at me and said, "Take that grass out of your mouth, Dad. You look like a hayseed."

Lost

JOSH WONDERED IF he should fire the shotgun. He put his hands on it, running his fingers down the grooves cut in the round, wooden pump. It was heavy. He could feel how heavy even now, with it resting on his legs. He had never been allowed to fire the gun, and now that he had carried it and learned how big it was, he did not want to. He wanted to be back with his brother.

Maybe Doug would let him carry the rifle, which had a sling. Then maybe they'd find the elk and Doug could shoot it and they could go home. He would like to see a dead elk. And he'd like to be there when Doug shot it, and not do anything wrong.

Josh looked around the clearing and down at the stump he sat on. Maybe Doug would see an elk and shoot right now. Then he would hear the shot and know where to go. There were some fallen, dying needles caught in the rough surface of the stump, and Josh picked them up and peeled them back to the base, pulling them into three parts. The resin stained his fingers.

He still couldn't recall how he had gotten here. He had tried so many directions to get back to Doug that he couldn't say for sure which way anything was now. He'd get in trouble for shooting the gun. If he told Doug he'd had to because he was lost, that would be worse. Doug said getting lost was the worst thing you could do.

Josh studied the trees, but they all looked the same, cold and dark, not at all like the ones outside the windows at home, where the chickadees came and ate the fat his mother hung from the branches. The trees here had all lost their lower branches, or they hung there dead. At home they were alive from the ground to as far as you could see. There weren't any chickadees up here either. Or anything else alive, except him. He wondered why Doug thought an elk would be up here. Maybe they were so big and lonely from people always shooting at them that they liked to live where nothing else did.

The snow wasn't falling hard. The flakes were enormous, but they came down more slowly than they should have been able to. It was simple to catch them on his tongue. But Josh knew being lost was bad and he started walking again, in a direction he thought he hadn't yet tried. When the trees were thin enough, he tilted his head back to catch another flake. It was so easy he couldn't waste all the chances. He could catch them and still keep walking.

Doug could find him even though the snow wasn't sticking. Doug was a great hunter. Doug could find him without snow, he bet, just by broken twigs and things. The ground was covered with twigs, though, most of them already broken. It might take Doug a long time. He hoped he'd already started. Doug would be mad when he found him, but it would be better than being by himself. He didn't know how the elk could stand it.

When he started to think about it, he got scared again. He didn't want to be here without Doug. Doug knew what to do here where nothing lived, but he didn't. He ran, as he had when he first realized he was lost. It made him tired, but he couldn't stop. He had to get back to Doug.

He didn't recognize anything that looked like where he'd searched for the grouse. Doug had told him he could follow the grouse, and if he found it to come back and get him. Then they'd see if they could kill it with a rock, so the noise of the gun wouldn't scare the elk. Doug had said he could throw the rock himself if they got close enough.

But he hadn't found the grouse, even though he'd looked on the ground and in the trees, just like Doug had told him. He hadn't found anything, and pretty soon he was just walking, no longer holding his breath in anticipation of the explosion of the grouse that had startled him so much the first time. Then when he couldn't find it and had turned around to go back to his brother, he found out he was lost and he had run, stumbling with the big gun, calling out Doug's name.

It was scary how little he could remember of following the grouse. He couldn't remember any of the trees or rocks or anything, even when he was still right there. And he'd wanted to remember everything about this day, the first time Doug took him hunting. He ran on, trying to think of a single thing he could remember, but the bad times came back more than anything else. Once, when he was sick, his mother put him to bed early, and he'd gotten mad. She had come into the dark room and slipped into the bed with him to make him feel better, but he had turned his back and held himself away from her. And now he was forgetting his whole life.

Josh continued to run and he held back his tears. Crying didn't do any good, Doug said, and Doug said he was too old to cry. The least he could do was not cry. He decided not to think of old things but vowed to remember more from then on. He stopped and memorized the trees that surrounded him, but it was so quiet he started running again, and he couldn't remember any trees after that. He didn't want to, either. He didn't like the trees anymore. And he didn't like the snow. It was coming harder now, and colder. It made everything look even more the same.

Doug had said that if he got lost to sit down and stay put. But he hadn't told him why, and it didn't make any sense to Josh. You could sit down forever and still not know where you were.

Doug had given him matches, too, saying they were the one thing you needed to have in the woods. He knew how to make a fire, but where would you build one? There weren't any grates or fire rings out here. What if he burned the whole forest down? He wouldn't build a fire until he had to. He wouldn't build a fire until it got dark.

The thought of still being lost when it got dark made Josh run even harder. He ran back up the hill to where he thought the clearing was. That was the last place he knew, and he would be closer to Doug there. He ran faster than he had ever run before, smashing the little twigs under his feet.

He didn't stop until he dropped the gun. He skidded to a halt then and looked at it, ready to run away. Doug had told him about guns going off when dropped, and Josh stood behind a tree waiting for it to shoot, hoping it would and that Doug would hear it and come find him. Then he would pretend he hadn't gotten lost but had just dropped the gun, like even hunters as good as Doug did sometimes. Then Doug would unload it for him and they could go home.

When the gun didn't go off, Josh crept back and sat down beside it. He touched the perfectly round barrel and remembered how fascinating it had always been in the gun cabinet at home. Now it was very cold, and so heavy his shoulders ached. Josh lay next to the gun and brushed the snow off. It was getting darker. He didn't know if it was just snowing harder or if night was coming. It must be almost night, he thought. It was getting that cold.

Josh sat up and wrapped his arms around his legs. He rocked slowly. He knew he had to build a fire. He knew Doug wasn't going to find him now, no matter what. The snow was sticking to the ground and Doug wouldn't be able to see the broken twigs. And not even Doug could find him in the dark. It was scary how dark it could get even when the snow made everything white.

Josh stood up and shivered. He wasn't afraid of the dark. It was nice to have light, though. The elk must be the saddest things in the world, he thought. They had to stay out every night in the dark with the snow falling right on them and sticking to them. Not the little ones, though, or the moms. They stayed together. It was only the bulls that had to stay way up here at night, alone.

Josh wasn't afraid of camping out either. He loved to do it with Doug. But even then it was quiet and kind of sad around the campfire, because you thought of other things you were missing and of your mom who never came with you but stayed at home by herself. That wouldn't be as bad, because she was in her house, with all the lights, but it was still sad to think of her by herself.

Josh shuffled through the woods, picking up little branches and breaking more off the dead, bottom parts of the trees. He wondered why the trees died at the bottoms but stayed alive at the top and kept growing up there. Maybe the trees forgot about their first branches when they got way up there. Maybe he'd grow up like that, forgetting everything that came first.

Josh was pretty sure he'd die tonight. It wasn't as scary as it had seemed when he'd been running without knowing where he was going. Pretty soon the trees wouldn't remember him anymore. They'd remember the elk sleeping out here by themselves, because the elk would still be doing it. He wasn't even sure if the live parts of the trees could see him anymore, it was getting so dark. Maybe they wouldn't remember him at all, not even for one night.

Josh returned to the gun and laid a branch of dead pine needles next to it. He stacked his twigs on top of that, then pulled the gun beside him and tried to light the needles. They weren't wet, but it took a lot of matches to get them to catch. The fire spread quickly to the twigs and then to the bigger branches Josh fed into it. It was good to have something to do, and it wasn't as lonely with the light. Soon the fire was warm, too, and Josh leaned toward it, holding his hands as close as he could.

It was completely dark now, and he thought about Doug driving back down all the dirt roads with the headlights bright on the road and everything so black and closed off beyond them. The radio would be on, too. It was so quiet around his little fire that Josh poked at it just to make the wood crackle. The woods around him were as black as the road beyond Doug's headlights.

When the coyote began to howl, so close to the fire, Josh couldn't hold back the tears. It wasn't crying so much. Just tears. He picked the gun out of the snow and brushed it off and laid it across his lap, even though it was cold where it touched him. He trembled as he found the trigger and put his finger next to it.

The coyote howled again, and tears rolled down Josh's cheeks. He thought of the elk all by himself in the dark with the snow piling up on his back without any way to get it off, and the coyotes that wanted to attack him from behind where he couldn't see them and tear out his guts while he was still standing. The elk never had a light at night or a fire to warm up with, or a gun to shoot the coyotes. He knew the elk didn't want to live up here, but that they had to because of people.

Josh held the gun up with his finger on the trigger. It was impossibly heavy, but he wanted to kill the coyote for the elk. He would leave the blasted carcass up here so the elk would find it. When the coyote called again, Josh got ready for it, squeezing the gun tight to himself like he'd seen Doug do. He was more stunned than hurt when it went off.

Josh dropped the gun and rolled away from where it had knocked him back. Doug was shouting at him from the darkness, and he knew he was in trouble, but he had never meant for the gun to shoot. Not until he had seen the coyote.

"Don't shoot, Josh!" Doug called from the darkness. "Don't shoot! I surrender!" He was laughing.

Josh squinted toward the voice and saw his brother move into the fire's ring of light. He was big and snow covered. Like the elk.

Josh stood up and whispered, "I didn't mean to shoot."

Doug came around the fire and knelt beside Josh, hugging him. "That was mean of me to howl. I was just kidding. I thought you'd know it was me. I've been looking for you all afternoon. You scared the hell out of me. Did you get lost?"

Josh shrugged. The snow that had piled up on his brother's fur cap touched his face. He remembered he'd been crying.

Doug let him go and stood to look at him. "I'm sorry I scared you. You just looked like such a mountain man sitting here by your fire in the middle of nowhere. Were you scared?"

Josh shrugged again. He wondered if the elk ever met at night, with their brothers maybe. If it was at night nobody would ever know, and so maybe they did.

"I'm proud of you, Josh," Doug told him. "I wouldn't have found you without this fire." He dropped off his pack and offered him a sandwich. "I bet you're hungry." He also took a grouse from the pack and held it up for Josh. "You scared him back to me. Do you want to cook him right now, over your fire?"

Josh did want to stay out here now, with Doug, knowing he wouldn't die. He watched the feathers Doug tore off the grouse drift around the flames and get sucked up by the heat, actually floating upward, into the darkness, up high to where the trees still remembered their branches.

He would like to forget about this day but remember eating the grouse with Doug around the fire he'd built by himself because he'd had to. And when Doug told him he'd almost had a shot at an elk, Josh didn't want to think about the elk being all alone in the dark, with the snow on him that he could not get off.

Harper

WHAT SPOOKED ME about Harper in the first place was this way he had of disappearing. In hunt camp he nearly faded out completely. But the two of us were always getting teamed up anyway, since I rarely brought a friend and no one seemed to claim Harper. We'd sidehill coulees for deer, each working one side till something kicked out the bottom. We'd try to stay pretty even, but half the time, well, most of the time, I'd lose sight of Harper. Even when he was working the open sides, with nothing but some ponderosa and snowberries for cover, even wearing orange, he'd just vanish.

Sitting down, I'd glass his side of the draw, knowing he had to be right across from me. I'd pick him out then, sliding along in his careful glide, head flicking this way and that, and the hair on my neck would stand up. Watching him slip wraithlike through the trees that way made me awfully glad Harper was on our side.

Once I asked Lance how many years he thought Harper'd been coming out. I thought he was Lance's friend, but Lance said he never saw him except on the hunts. "And half the time not then," he added. Neither of us could remember when he'd first shown up.

At night, crowded into the tent, Harper found the shadows. With the stories going around you'd swear he wasn't there at all, until somebody'd say that rare thing that'd trigger a story out of Harper. The whole tent would go quiet then, as if a stranger had walked in, and we'd listen to Harper talk.

Later all I'd remember of his stories was his voice, flitting through the smoke like the aspen leaves behind our rushing trucks. That was fall, I always thought—that yellowy dance in the rearview. And that's what Harper got to seem: a shadowy incarnation of fall, of brittle leaves and crackling air, the blue sky's first paling.

So, when we put together our first-ever spring hunt, for bear, I guessed Harper wouldn't appear. None of us had any idea what to do with a bear, but getting out after being holed up all winter seemed like a pretty good idea. The week before the season, Lance and I brought a worn-out nag from his ranch up to our elk spot. Poor old girl could barely totter to where we planned to use her for bait, and I didn't feel as bad as I thought I would when Lance put her down.

Bouncing back down the ruts, though, with the horse trailer rattling so empty behind us, I asked Lance if he thought Harper would show. Lance said, "Not a doubt. Don't we just fold him up with the tent every fall?"

I laughed but said, "Wouldn't be surprised if we did. Doesn't he give you the creeps?"

Lance laughed harder, asking what I was talking about. He always hunted with his son, so I told him what it was like being out in the hills with Harper. "I can't stand the way he vanishes," I told Lance. "Into hillsides with nothing but grass."

"He's a spook all right."

"Maybe he won't show," I said. "I've never seen him except in the fall."

"Maybe not," Lance answered, not really listening. He worked the trailer over a cattle guard, and we dropped back down to the valley.

By the time the season opened, Lance and the rest of them had camp set up, but work held me late and I was the last one there. Coming through the tent flap I looked for Harper first thing, and for a moment I thought I was in the clear, but then I saw him, back in the corner, smiling and nodding his greeting while the others shouted and laughed, already replaying new legends from last fall. I nodded back at Harper, quiet enough on his cot that I wondered again if he hadn't been there all winter and was just now starting to thaw.

There was at least one bear working the horse, they told me, maybe more. With six of us, we couldn't all sit on the bait, so we'd take turns, pairing up, two in the morning, two in the evening. During the day, we'd nap or walk the hills, hunting without bait. Sure enough, Harper and I had already been matched up.

We drew the first evening shift on the bait, what everybody expected to be the best chance, but Harper wasn't the same as in the fall. Cramped together in the little wickiup blind, he couldn't stop fidgeting. For the first time ever I wasn't afraid he'd disappear any second. I was more worried that he was so obviously here he might blow our chances.

After we'd been in the blind for nearly an hour, Harper whispered, "Doesn't seem much like hunting, does it?"

"What's that?" I asked, startled to hear him speak at all.

"Sitting here over a rotting horse."

I shrugged. "I suppose our chances are a lot better here than out in the woods."

"I suppose," he whispered, unconvinced, easing back to lean against the aspen that made up the rear of the blind.

We'd tramped the hills all day together without coming closer to a bear than crossing piles of their droppings, and I was tired, having to concentrate on watching the horse just to keep from dozing. The time was right for bears—the night closing down fast, the breeze advertising our bait all down the mountain. But I could barely keep awake, and I rubbed at my eyes, forcing myself to focus on the horse's ear, which stood upright as if still listening for approaching menace. I whispered, "That bear doesn't get here quick, I'll be snoring," but Harper didn't answer. When I turned to see if he'd nodded off, he wasn't there.

I shivered, whispering, "God, I hate that," and turned back to look at the horse and whatever else might be out there now.

In the next few minutes the colors faded out of everything, and I guessed I had about three minutes of shooting light left. I shifted my weight around, loosening up, getting ready to go. The flashlight was with me and I thought, *Too bad for Harper, he can find his own way back.* Damn spook.

When I glanced back up, the bear was only a few feet from the horse, his head up high, nose working the air like a dog. Through the scope, even with the usual hum of buck fever, I noticed the heavy droop of his lower lip, as if he was in a sulk about something. I put the crosshairs on his neck, just down from the ear, and followed as he lowered his head to the horse. I eased in a breath and pulled the trigger just before he took his first bite.

The bear flipped over backwards, as if knocked there by the shot, though I doubted the bullet could have that much force. I held still a moment, watching the tired-looking stretch straighten his legs, the only motion he made after landing on his back like that. Slowly I lowered my rifle. I thought, *You've got yourself a bear. First one ever.* Then I thought, *So what?* The shot had been like sighting in a rifle. I wasn't seventy-five yards away.

I circled around to the bait in the dark and wondered where in the world Harper was. Peeking over the horse I saw that the black bear was smaller than I'd have guessed—nothing like the salmon-eating Kodiaks I'd watched on television. But a white V marked his chest, and I realized the hide would actually be fairly handsome. His head was tilted to the side, his lips both dangling away from the teeth like a sleeping hound's.

The air was pretty ripe this close to the old horse, and I grabbed one of the bear's legs to drag him upwind. Tightening my grip, I felt the softer fur beneath the long, coarse hair. Then I thought I heard something, a rustling nearby, and I stood straight up, getting that odd Harper-shiver down my spine. But there was nothing there, nothing I could see, anyway, and I bent back down and wrestled the bear out of the stink.

I did the gutting by flashlight, which was frustrating enough that I actually wished Harper hadn't bugged out on me. But Lance had a plastic sled in the blind and I rolled the bear onto it, and the trip back to the tent was easy, even exciting on the last downhill stretch. The sled crashing into a tree beside the tent alerted everyone inside, and soon the lantern was out and we had the bear hung in no time.

It was warm enough that we decided to skin it right then. Even with all the advice the skinning went pretty fast, and once we had the hide rolled, we moved back into the tent for dinner and drinks.

All through the skinning everybody'd been waiting for the story of the hunt. I kept telling them there wasn't one, but with the drinks they insisted, so I told them every detail, which took about two seconds, leaving out the part about Harper vanishing.

So, instead of the usual post-kill stories, we were all left standing there holding on to our cups, the fire popping against the sides of the stove. I felt them looking at me, expecting me to go on, but the story was done. "That's all," I said. "He walked up and I shot him."

I saw them look down at the ground, and I said, "Then I zinged him down here on Lance's sled," because it was the only thing I could think to add. I told how the sled ran over me at one point and got a few laughs, but that was all. Silence.

Then from Harper's cot came that dry, old-leaf voice, saying, "You should have seen it," and everyone turned away from me toward his gloomy corner.

"Should have seen that bear rolling up the mountain, all big-butted, nose in the air like there was a string attached. Pausing now and then, sniffing around, testing the wind, knowing something was wrong, but not quite able to resist old Nell.

"Right to where he can see Nell, and he gets a whiff of human. Turns on his heel. Charges three or four steps straight back down the mountain but hauls up short and thinks it over. Pretty soon he starts pacing back and forth, eventually pointing back up to Nell, working his way a little closer each step.

"Could practically see him argue it out, weighing the pros and cons.

"Finally he just says, 'The hell with it, it's been a long winter and I'm starving,' and starts in for Nell with that towed-by-a-string look again, and no sooner does he drop his head than Wham! He's down and out, and Donny here's blowing smoke from his barrel."

When Harper stopped talking the tent went quiet again. Lance cleared his throat and said, "Her name was Belle. Not Nell," and Harper didn't say anything to that.

Somebody else asked, "How'd you see all that from the blind?"

"He wasn't in the blind," I said, and everyone turned back to me. "He disappeared about half an hour before."

"How did you know all that?" I asked Harper.

Harper's voice was even softer than usual, practically mumbling. "Followed him up the hill," he said.

I looked at Lance and shook my head, and Lance, who'd had the fruitless morning shift on the bait, said, "Never thought of chasing them to the bait," and everybody laughed. Pretty soon somebody mentioned dinner, and we jumped on the change of subject.

After eating I went out to check on the bear, actually just to look at him, hoping I could think of something to do with him. Picturing his winter, living off his own fat, and remembering the stink of old Belle he'd found so tantalizing, I wasn't that interested in eating him.

The naked bear was hanging from one front paw, and in the dim light cast through the white canvas of the tent he looked strangely human—the arms and ribs looking like I guessed my own would flayed. I touched the meat, finding it cooler than I'd expected. I pushed against the carcass, setting it swinging. Out of the blackness Harper said, "So, you got him."

I leapt back, pulling my hand from the bear as if I'd been burned. "Christ almighty, you scared the shit out of me!" I said, looking all through the darkened woods without finding a trace of Harper.

"Sorry," he said. "Didn't mean to do that. I thought you'd know it was me."

"Of course I know it's you." *Who else would be skulking out here*, I thought. "I just wasn't expecting you." I peered into the growing blackness. "For crying out loud, where are you?"

Then Harper was there, standing on the other side of the bear. The light really was bad and he was tough to make out.

"Where'd you disappear to up there?" I asked, still startled, sounding more peevish than I meant to. "You should've seen me trying to hold the light and gut him myself."

"Couldn't take that blind anymore," Harper answered.

"Decided to look for him on my own." Harper reached up and shook the bear's paw, as if finally introducing himself. "Found this one moving in on the scent and followed him in. I knew you'd take him."

I realized that if he was following the bear I could have shot right at him. "You should have said something. I didn't know where you were."

Harper just shrugged and I asked, "Why didn't you take him? If you were so close?"

Harper let the bear's paw drop. "What would I do with a bear?"

"I don't know," I said. "I was just trying to figure out the same thing." I tried laughing, but Harper didn't answer. "Why are you out here then, if you aren't going to shoot anything?" I asked.

"Don't have any idea. Thought it might be as good as the fall. But sitting over a dead horse named Belle isn't anything like the fall," Harper said, his voice still whispering along like a breath through dead leaves.

"It gets us out here," I answered, already aware that wasn't enough.

"True," Harper whispered. "But it doesn't get us stalking. It doesn't get us seeing what's here and what's there and what it all means." He let out a long breath. "Why bother coming out if there's not that?"

"I know," I answered, thinking of how I'd felt watching the bear flip over. "Are you going out tomorrow? Not over the bait, but hunting?"

In the dark I could just barely see Harper nod and I asked, "Mind if I go with you? Just to watch."

"To see what you can see? Sure."

Then Harper must have taken a step backward, out of the light, because he wasn't there in front of me anymore. He wasn't there at all. In the darkness all I could see besides the eerily human naked bear was the whirl of yellow leaves, settling down after our passing rush.

Home Before Dark

My stepson, Gordon, was already in the cafe when I got there, and he poured coffee for me as I sat down. He added my cream and sugar without asking, though sugar was something I'd given up a long time ago. I stared at him while he stirred the cream. We'd had dinner the night before, with our wives, but I'd spent the night watching Sandy, my wife—his mom—worried about how she was holding up.

We ordered a quick breakfast, and because I couldn't think of anything to say, I asked, "When's the last time you went fishing?"

"Years ago. Monique isn't much of an outdoorsman. I wish she would have come, though. She was pretty nervous last night. But, you'd like her if you got to know her."

"I'm sure of that," I said conversationally, but Gordon gave me a quick glance, a questioning look I remembered. "If you picked her to stick with she must be a good one," I said, and it sounded as false as it was.

Gordon said, "You're the one who picked well."

"I tried to get your mom to come along," I told him. "But she thought it would be nice if just the two of us went."

"Old time's sake."

I nodded, though Sandy had stayed home thinking I might get some answers out of him alone. We looked away from each other as the food was set down. After the waitress left, I took a deep breath but wound up only asking something harmless, like "What have you been doing?" or "Where'd you and Monique meet?"

And Gordon responded with the same light chatter. We argued over the bill when it came, and I didn't mention his mother again until we were taking the canoe off the car, explaining that Sandy and I had run the shuttle last night. After we settled the canoe into the river, Gordon stood beside it, staring out over the flow of dark water. Dawn was late with the fall, and it was just growing light. Scattered flocks of geese struggled by overhead, barely visible, honking mournfully. The air was much colder than it had been yesterday, wafer-thin ice rimming the stones against the bank.

"Thanks for showing this to me again," Gordon said, shivering, huddling deeper into his coat. If it'd been years and years ago, I would've run my hands up and down his sides, quick and hard, chasing away goose bumps. But I just stood quietly on the bank and watched him shiver.

"Ready?" I asked.

"And waiting," he answered, his old line.

I paddled from the stern, and Gordon was quick to strip out line and begin casting. But he was wearing big, goofy mittens, city things, and it was nearly impossible for him to hold his line. He laughed about it, and I asked if he wanted my fingerless gloves.

He shook his head without turning around and said, "I've just got to toughen up is all. I've forgotten about so much." He took off his mittens then and started casting for real. I'd forgotten how graceful he was, and I stopped paddling to watch him quarter the nymph upstream and work it across the current.

"You haven't forgotten a thing," I said.

"That's not what I expected to hear from you," he responded. He did turn then, his old challenging smile bold across his face.

"Forgotten a thing about fishing," I explained.

He waited for me to go on, his smile starting to quaver the way it did when he was in trouble as a kid, trying so hard to show he didn't care. I watched him turn away, picking up his rod, and I told myself again that I was glad to see him, glad to see him hug his mother again. But I also knew I'd never be able to forget how he'd just disappeared, how he'd left her wondering for six years. During those years I'd never doubted that we'd see him again, and I kept reassuring Sandy, whispering things about adolescent rage, the difficulties of leaving the nest, the whole time picturing that smug smile of his, wondering if I'd be able to keep from punching it from his face when he reappeared.

He had a strike then, and I've rarely been so happy to see one. His face lit up, and he lifted the rod tip just quickly enough to set the hook without pulling it away. The trout was a native, a cutthroat, not too big, and it gave up quickly. Gordon dipped his hand into the icy water, freeing the hook, releasing the fish just as I said, "Awful nice pan size."

He looked down into the water. "I never liked killing them," he said.

"What are you talking about? We ate rivers of trout. Your mom loves them."

"That was before I knew there were so many ends to things."

Gordon looked at me, and I was shocked by the startling familiarity of his face. I remembered the odd gold bursts flecking his brown eyes. When he was a boy they'd bothered me. They were a flaw, I thought, somehow eerie. They were too light, like sheep's eyes.

Suddenly he squinted, and I knew he was smiling his real smile. "I got the first. The biggest. The smallest. The most. I'm killing you in every category."

I'd forgotten the old contests we'd developed in the years I'd tried to gentle into his father's place. "Give me time," I said, and Gordon stripped up his slack and cast again.

We both fished as much as we could, but nothing else struck before the river curved and I had to put down my rod for my paddle. Gordon retrieved his nymph, too, but instead of picking up a paddle to help, he stuck his hands under his arms.

"It's funny how whenever I thought about all this it was always the fish I remembered, and the way the river looked when the mist was just clearing. Or the way you'd get so tense going through whitewater, how it wasn't safe to say anything then, but afterward whatever I said was the funniest thing in the world. It was never the damn cold I remembered."

I glanced at the bottom of the canoe, the same one we'd used then. After he'd left I'd been able to forget he'd ever been with me, that he'd ever seen that kind of thing with me.

"It's never the damn cold I remember," Gordon said again, arms still wrapped tight around himself. "Or lugging all our stuff over those endless portages. Or sitting under the canoe during the downpours—blackfly bait."

"No one remembers the bad stuff," I said, realizing even as I spoke that that's exactly what I'd forced myself to remember about Gordon. "Why would anyone bother remembering that?"

"I think if you don't you'll wind up crazy," he answered, taking his hands out from under his arms and blowing on his fingers. "I can't even feel my fingers," he said. "You'd think I'd remember anything that hurt this much."

"It's your mind's trick. Blocking out the bad."

"It's a dirty trick," Gordon said, picking up his rod, his mom's rod, which I'd brought for him to use. He turned away from me, casting again. "If all you remember is the good, you wind up homesick for things that really weren't that great to begin with."

We were on another flat, quiet stretch, and I picked up my rod to change flies. The knot I tied took concentration. "It really was pretty great," I said quietly, beginning to understand how he'd worked things around after he left, worked them around so he could stand himself.

Gordon shrugged, facing away from me, and then nodded quickly. I could picture how he'd bite his lower lip, exactly how his cheeks would be sucked in just a little, the tightness of the lines around his golden eyes. If there wasn't the full distance of the canoe between us, I might have crawled forward then, to hug him or swat some sense into him, I wasn't sure which. But it would be dangerous now, even in the flat water, to try to make my way to him.

When Gordon had his line in, he cast out again, quartering upstream expertly. I doubted he'd forgotten a thing, no matter what he said. I began casting, too, pulling my line in whenever we reached a bend I'd have to steer through. We both started to catch fish, and I saved a few for Sandy.

The day never did warm the way it should have and when we stopped for lunch I started a little fire. While I was building it up, when it still needed my help to keep burning, Gordon fished the hole just upstream. The glaze-thin ice had never melted off, and though there was no sun, the ice glinted white at the edge of the riffles, where the water did not move fast enough to break it.

Gordon worked the riffle, bouncing his nymph along the bottom through the broken water. I watched him pick up a fish with his first cast, then I went back to working on the fire. The next time I looked he had another fish on. His breath smoked into the pinching air.

When the fire had taken hold solidly, I sat beside it to watch Gordon fish. I studied him a long time, trying again to picture the sullen look of hatred we'd never understood—the look I'd thought was directed at me for replacing his father, that Sandy had thought was for her for ever divorcing in the first place. He was intent on his fishing, and he kept at it a long while without turning to see that he was being watched. He seemed to have worked the hole out, though, and he didn't hook anything else.

Maybe it was the overcast, blocking the arc of the sun, that hid the slipping away of the day, but I sat by that fire far too long watching Gordon, while the day, and our light, kept getting shorter, the river still stretching out before us.

Finally he reeled his line in and walked back to the fire, draping three trout over the log I was sitting on. "Let's eat," he said.

He caught me looking at the dead fish and he said, "You've killed three too. Now you can save them for Mom. She loves them."

I couldn't tell if the fish were a peace offering or if he was making fun of my murderous ways. I told him we'd save his for Sandy, and I picked up my beautifully clean little trout, and we roasted them straight over coals we dragged from the main body of the fire. We ate with our fingers, and Gordon said he hadn't tasted anything like that in years. Even then, when I knew we had to get moving, we stayed over the fire, unable to draw away from its warmth, from the mesmerizing dance of the flames.

As Gordon watched the fire, I finally asked the question neither Sandy nor I had been able to manage the night before. After all, we were on the river now, and there was no place he could run. "What brings you back, Gordon?" I whispered.

Gordon didn't look up from the fire. For a long time he didn't answer. "Monique, I guess. She started it, anyway." He looked up then and smiled for a moment. "I'm glad she did, though. Some things get to seem way harder than they really are."

Somehow that shy, little smile did all the wrong things, and the urge to reach across the fire and wipe it off his mouth welled up. "Six years is an awful long time," I said. "Without a word."

Gordon nodded and looked back into the last of the flames. "I know."

"We didn't even know if you were still alive. You about killed Sandy."

Gordon nodded again, a quick, guilty dip of his head. "When I left I thought that's what she was doing to me."

I looked away from him then, and when neither of us could say any more, I walked down to the canoe for the bailing bucket. I filled it in the river and came back to douse the fire.

"We're late," I said, too fast, trying to cut him off before he could say anything else. "We stayed here too long."

"How much farther do we have to go?"

"A long way."

The water hit the fire with a screaming hiss, and great clouds of steam poured up, mixing with the leaden sky. Gordon stirred the ashes with a stick, and I poured on a second bucket. "It's dead now," he said.

"We've got to move, Gordon. We're going to have a hell of a time making it home before dark."

He nodded but stood still over the blackened sticks, watching the last of the steam trickling up. "That's what Mom always used to say. Remember that? 'Be sure to be home before dark.'"

I nodded. "She never said it much to me," I said.

"She didn't have to," he started, but before he said anything else, he pointed into the sky. "More geese."

I looked up at the tired, ragged Vs, low with the clouds. "Looking for a place to spend the night," I said.

"Already heading south?"

"It's getting that late. So are we."

"They sound sad to be leaving," Gordon said, walking to the canoe.

I held the canoe steady in the current while he climbed in. I pushed off and started paddling. "We really are late," I told him. "We've got to move."

Gordon picked up his paddle and started to put his back into it. I made some comment about his strength, and he started in on what his workout schedule was and all that. It was exactly the kind of mindless, friendless chitchat I'd been afraid of miring down in all day.

But Gordon stopped in midsentence, as if he'd been thinking the same thing. "Do both the geese raise their young? The male and the female?" he asked.

I opened my mouth to answer, but then guessed it really wasn't a question so much. I said, "I don't know," and we both paddled hard, watching the clouds dropping even lower, hiding the mountains the sun was setting behind.

We kept up the power as dusk wrapped around us, working too hard to speak. And then the snow began to fall, tiny white touches against our faces. "Warm enough?" I asked, and Gordon said he was fine. The snow grew steady, patient at its task, bringing on the dark even more quickly. "Are we going to get out of here before dark?" Gordon asked.

"Not a chance," I answered, thinking of Sandy watching the snow and the clock.

"What are we going to do?"

"Keep going, I guess. The river's pretty easy." But I followed the river's curves in my mind, through the looping **S** just before the takeout. I told Gordon about it. "There are three snags in it. Upstream one in the center, next one left, last one right. It's not hard in the light."

"Can we reach it before dark?"

"I don't know." I felt the canoe push forward a little harder with Gordon's next stroke, and I put my back into my own paddling. I knew we wouldn't make it.

Our eyes kept searching through less and less light, until finally we were guessing at shadows. Soon I realized I was listening for the bank more than trying to see it.

We both stopped paddling for a moment. "Should we get out and walk?" Gordon asked.

"I don't have a light," I said, trying to remember if I'd ever forgotten to bring one before. "We'd probably get lost. At least I know where the river goes."

I could hear Gordon cut his wooden blade into the water, and we began to paddle again, my ears straining against the blinding darkness.

"Is this dumb?" Gordon asked. "Are we going to kill ourselves out here tonight?"

"Of course it's dumb."

"I knew it would be," he said, but then I began to hear a faint rise in the hissing of the water. I said, "We may be there." I reached out with my paddle and it touched against the bank.

Gordon said, "The snags?"

The hiss was a rushing sound now, and I said, "Yes. If you can see the first one, go hard left after it."

"I can't see a thing."

"Well, hear. If you can hear it."

We were quiet then, and the rushing grew louder. It seemed to be in the right place. I held my paddle out to the bank once more, measuring, remembering the snags. The blade scraped harshly against the gravel, and the air around us erupted.

The explosion of honking startled me so badly it was a moment before I realized they were geese, hundreds of them struggling up from the banks. The wind whistled and whisked through their wings. Their honking battered my ears, as if they screamed warnings, unable to believe I couldn't hear. I thought if I reached up perhaps they would lift me off this river, over the snags ahead.

I felt Gordon pulling hard to the left up front, and though I could hear nothing but the geese, I drew hard that way. Then the canoe brushed something on the right, lifting and listing, and I thought we were going over. There was a flash of lighter water on that side and the canoe righted itself, and we were through before I knew we'd started. The geese and the rush of water faded behind us, and I could hear Gordon breathing hard up front.

"Did we make it?" he whispered. "Were those the snags?"

"Those were the snags."

"We hit the last one, didn't we?"

"Grazed it."

"Are there any more? Was that the last of it?"

"That's all," I said, my heart only now beginning to speed up, battering at my ribs as I pictured the two of us tumbling alone through the black, ice-bound current.

Gordon said something else, but we broke through another flock of geese. They sounded as if they were in the boat, and I could feel individual birds going over my head. Once I heard the hard flutter of braking wings, and a heavy gust of air hit my cheek. When they faded downstream, Gordon said, "One of them touched me. On the face."

"I thought they were going to carry us away."

"What will they do now? How will they land in the dark?"

"I don't know."

"They don't have to keep flying until it gets light, do they?"

He sounded so distressed I said, "No," though I didn't have any idea what they could or could not do. "They can land at night. They can feel how close they are to the ground."

"Really?" he asked, and I said, "Sure."

"I wish I could've done that," he said, and we kept moving downriver, occasionally touching the banks with our paddles to make sure we were still there. Gordon said it was like floating through space, and if he couldn't touch the bank, he wouldn't even know he was on the planet. "Maybe we didn't make it through the snags. Maybe this is our afterlife."

"No," I said. "We wouldn't be here without your mom. I wouldn't be."

"Or Monique," he said. "Monique would be with me."

I waited for him to say, "And Mom," but he didn't do that. I said, "What did you think about when we started to tip back there? Who did you think about?"

"Monique," he answered, too fast, before he could have given it any thought. Then he blurted, "She's pregnant. That's what I thought about. That's why she made me come here to see Mom."

I didn't say anything. I'd wanted him to say Sandy, but I could see now why that wouldn't be true.

Then Gordon said, "That's all I ever think about now. I walk around scared to death. Scared about things I'd never even thought of."

I laughed a little, vengefully, but Gordon ignored me. "Does that ever leave? Even when you've taken all the tests? Even when you know the baby is all right? Isn't the fear supposed to go away?"

The moon had come up behind the clouds and I could see the faintest outline of Gordon against the sky, and I told him that the fear goes away, although I really didn't know much about it. Gordon was my only experience at being a parent, and he'd been ten years old when we'd met. But I remembered getting up on nights as dark as this to stand in his doorway, listening for his breathing, and I doubted that the fear ever disappeared completely. No test was that foolproof.

"Why won't mine go away, then? My fear?"

"Maybe it changes more than goes away. Becomes more awe than fear."

"Just the thought of being a dad scares me," Gordon whispered. "What if you do your best and they turn out like me?"

There was no answer for that, and we paddled until suddenly the takeout was there, appearing as quickly as the water cut by the snags. I pulled over, and the canoe scraped the gravel. I said, "End of the line."

Gordon stayed in his seat. I could see his outline in the river now, the water holding the light of the clouds. I held my hand out. I don't know how he saw it in the dark, but he took it and I pulled him up out of the canoe. Once he was on the bank, we let go of each other.

"We've got to move. We're probably scaring Sandy to death."

We picked up the canoe and carried it toward my truck. "Does she worry about you now? Does she tell you to be home before dark?" Gordon asked.

"Of course," I said. "She loves me."

"So there's nothing left for you to fear, is there?"

"Losing that."

"Doesn't that scare you to death? All by itself?"

"No," I said, wondering if that was true. "You can't start missing the greatest thing in the world before it's even gone." I paused, trying to remember his words. "You'd wind up crazy if you did that."

We lifted the canoe onto the truck, and when I walked around for the tiedowns I bumped into Gordon in the dark. I felt the sticky touch of the fish he'd killed for his mother. He stepped quickly backwards and I could feel him staring at me. "She'll love those fish," I said.

"I'm sorry," he said. "About leaving. About everything. I was such a mess then."

His words brushed against my face like the startled rush of a goose wing. I told him his mother had known that all along but that if he could bring himself to tell her, it would be like one of those wondrous tests they had now, the ones Monique had taken, that really assured nothing, but meant so much anyway.

Side Show

THE CRAWL, WHICH HAD STARTED out looking so simple, had grown ridiculous. From the highway, with the flakes flashing by in a dizzying rush, the snow had not looked this wet. Crawling, it soaked through Marianne's elbows and knees in a matter of seconds and brushed off on her back and dripped onto her neck. And the trail itself, overgrown and hostile with thorns from years of battling cattle, grew smaller and smaller, until finally Marianne had to admit she was following a rabbit run. Derek, she guessed, was sitting in the car with the radio on, dry and laughing.

When she'd told him to stop the car, lifting her binoculars at the same time, she hadn't been able to keep the excitement out of her voice. "Geese!" she exclaimed. "Look at all of them."

Derek had said, "We're after deer today, Marianne."

"But, geese. I've only ever seen ducks there."

The geese lined the shore of the little island, hunkered down in the thick snowfall. "I've jumped ducks there before. It's a cakewalk." That was very nearly true, Marianne thought now. She'd jumped them at the head of the island, not the tail, but looking at it from five hundred yards, the difference hadn't seemed worth mentioning.

Once they'd recrossed the bridge and had driven back up to the island, she took out her shotgun and loaded quickly. "It'll only take a second. Really. We'll get after your deer as soon as I'm done," she told him, then waved and dropped down the road berm and scampered across the rocks and shallows to the head of the island, the dense growth hiding her from the geese, making everything simple.

Now, shifting her gun around a knot of wild rose before crushing over it herself, the stickers piercing the forearm of her coat, she couldn't believe how tangled the tail of the island was. This was taking a lot longer than she had guessed, and she wondered if Derek was still laughing.

He didn't like ducks, and she wasn't sure geese were much higher up on his list. They didn't often run across geese. He liked the vast return of big-game hunting. "One shot—season of eating," he'd tell her. "And no plucking."

That was exactly the problem, Marianne thought: One shot—end of season. With birds, there was shot after shot after shot, and Marianne couldn't understand why he wouldn't see that.

She tried to move more quickly, but the ceiling of her trail wasn't a foot tall and she wasn't crawling now, she was slithering. The snow soaked through her wool, and she wondered if she'd freeze later, up in the hills chasing after mule deer.

Finally Marianne's trail just stopped. In front of her was some sort of blowdown, a tangle of rose and hawthorn, alder and willow, the branches crushed down horizontally. She caught her breath a moment, then tried to crawl over it.

The river, gray and cold, rustled by only ten yards to her right, and she winced at the overwhelming crackling and snapping of her movements. She guessed the geese were beside her now, and she studied the branches between her and the river, figuring that if she stood, if the blown down bushes would hold her weight, she'd have a fairly clear field of fire.

The creeping limbs grabbed at her feet as she tried to ready them beneath her, and she had to use her hands to free them. With her gun lying in the snow beside her, she wondered that the geese didn't flush right now. They usually managed something diabolical like that. All her life she hadn't shot more than two or three geese.

Finally Marianne stood, crouched at first, moving up slowly as she looked at more and more water. Suddenly, still too far downstream, she saw the geese, and she dropped back down like a stone. She hadn't been seen, and the geese were still sticking to the shoreline, dejected looking, careless in the miserable weather.

Once back into the tangle, Marianne couldn't see any way to proceed. There appeared to be a trail ahead of her, but walking across the blowdown wasn't working, her feet slipping through, the matted branches clutching at her as if deliberately trying to hold her back.

Marianne smiled, glad Derek wasn't here to see this. She took the shells from her shotgun, held it against her chest, and started to roll across the branches. The constant rustle seemed less threatening than the thunder of each footstep, and soon she was across the tangle. The new trail was another rabbit run, but after the blowdown it looked like an interstate. She reloaded and began to slither forward again.

Soon she could hear the geese, quiet murmurs, none of the blatant honking she knew would fill the air when she stood. She looked for the single cottonwood she'd marked the geese with from the road, but from the thickets on the island she could see nothing.

She found a thinner spot in the forest of choking branches and tried bulling her way toward the river. The noise was appalling, and she thought she heard a lone, questioning honk. The brush reached nearly seven feet high here, and on tiptoe she knew she wouldn't break six. But she was practically on the river's edge, and Marianne knew she was running out of options.

She got off her stomach and snaked a leg forward, parting the branches with the barrels of her shotgun, so she'd at least be able to lift it if they spooked. Slowly she stood to her full height, but she could see no geese. She couldn't see the shore either, and she realized she was on the top of a cutbank. The geese had to be below her, not ten yards away, maybe not even five. Either that or they'd swum downstream. If they'd done that, she'd give up. Derek wouldn't wait forever.

Crouching, Marianne took another step forward. She was able to see the lip of the drop-off and she reached forward with her elbows, hooking the last of the branches and pulling them behind her as she took her final step, already bringing her gun up to her shoulder.

She had to look down to see the geese, thick on the shore-line, staring at her, not moving other than to stretch their necks in surprise. Marianne said, "Gotcha," and the bank exploded in a roar of honking as the geese blew out over the water, dead away from Marianne.

She was so close she waited, swinging with one of the first geese up, holding, holding, then easing back on the trigger. The goose somersaulted over and Marianne was already swinging to the left, picking up the next goose in the line. She fired quickly, and that goose crumpled too.

Marianne dropped her gun low enough to reload, just notic-ing the goose behind her second kill falter, stagger on a wing-tip, then set its wings and crash out near the middle of the river. Its neck came up instantly, and it began to paddle away from her, to the far bank.

As she lifted her gun again, sighting down at that long neck in the water, Marianne was already beginning to think, "Three geese! Three geese in one jump! Three geese with two shots!" She shot, and the third goose's neck folded and it began to drift downstream, head down in the water.

"Three geese!" Marianne whispered out loud. "And he called this a side show."

The air was still full of geese, and ducks had lifted off from somewhere too, whistling through the air above her. Marianne dropped in another shell and crouched down. She glanced at her geese, all with their heads down, drifting, and she waited to see if any ducks would make a mistake.

But the commotion began to die down, and nothing flew into range. Marianne kept glancing at her geese. She was dressed for deer hunting, not goose, and she began to wonder how she would retrieve the birds without waders. She broke onto the shore and trotted downstream, thinking she could catch the closest pair at the very end of the island. With any luck they'd even eddy out in the shallows.

The wind was stronger than she'd thought, though, and by the time Marianne reached the end of the island, the geese had already passed the shallows and were beginning to hook around the bend.

The shallow here was deeper than at the head of the island, over her boot tops for sure. She should have run to the top of the island to cross back over, but if she did that now, the geese would be long gone. She sat down quickly and tore at the laces of her boots. Stuffing her wool socks into the boots, she rolled her pants up as far as she could and stepped into the backwater at the tail of the island.

Her feet quickly went numb, but even so the pain was sharp. She began to run, lifting her feet high, trying not to splash herself. Once across she hustled over the snow-covered rocks until she was downstream of the geese. The water was moving here, deeper than she'd hoped, blackened by the overcast, endlessly pocked by the falling snow. She left her shotgun on the bank and stepped in, the current feeling nearly warm after the snow.

She moved out until the water reached her rolled-up cuffs, but the geese were still a step farther out, maybe even two steps, drifting on quickly. The other goose was way out, hopelessly beyond her reach, and she couldn't begin to think how she'd retrieve it. She considered running back to shore and stripping off her pants, but behind her was a big hole, way over her head, and she took another step out.

The black water reached the middle of her thigh, soaking her pants. She glanced down at her legs, then back up at the geese. She took another step, realizing the bottom was sliding down deeper and deeper. The water reached her waist, and she knew the deer hunt was over.

The weight of her sodden clothes began to pull at her like something alive. She held her arms out to her sides, bit her lip, and took one more step, beginning to stretch forward for the geese, standing on tiptoe without realizing it.

The water coiled around her chest and her breathing lost its rhythm. She panted, choking in strangling gasps, the strain creasing her face, making her squint. She dipped forward, grasping a hand around the neck of each goose at the same time.

She swung the geese up, surprised for an instant by their weight, and she turned for shore in the same instant, the way a retriever would, turning even as it scooped the bird into its mouth.

But all in that same instant, the geese came to life. Their wings spread out from their heavy bodies and they began to flap. Not weakhearted nerve tremors, but the full-fledged thrashing of adult geese, as if they were trying to lift her off the river themselves. Marianne wondered, at the end of the instant, if she hadn't seen the tops of their black bills out of the water, the nostrils free in the air, the shiny black eyes watching her, waiting for her to step in just too far.

Then the first blow connected. The hard, bony bend of elbow struck Marianne just under the eye, showing her stars, and she scowled as she squeezed her fingers as tightly as she could around the feathered necks and tried to find her way back to shore.

She squeezed and shook her fists, her feet scrabbling over river rock she could no longer feel. She ducked her head, shielding her face from the rain of blows. She was still chest-deep, and she couldn't lift the geese free of the water. Each slashing blow was slowed by the water, but the spray was blinding and freezing, and Marianne closed her eyes until she fought her way to waist-deep water.

Then she tried to twirl the birds, tried to spin them around her fists until their necks broke. But the geese flapped their wings, righting themselves before she could complete a single circle.

Finally Marianne heaved one of the birds away from her toward shore. She grabbed the second and spun it, twirled it as if she were a hammer thrower. She thought she felt the sudden looseness as the neck vertebrae separated, and she hurled it after the first.

She was gasping wildly for breath, numb from her chest down, stumbling for shore, water streaming from her hair into her eyes, blinding her, when she met the first goose, swimming back out to her. She stumbled over it, wrapping it with her chest and arms, holding it underwater until she reached the shore. Then she picked up a rock and began to beat its head, over and over, until she caught her own finger between the stones and cried out.

On her hands and knees, Marianne hunched over the mangled goose and sucked in great, heaving breaths. Then she began to shiver. She stuck her feet into her boots, picked up her geese and shotgun, and started to cut across the small field to their car, stumbling as she went, blinking back the water that continued to dribble from her hair.

When she reached the road, she let the geese fall and tried to trot to the car. Derek was pointed away from her, and she could see his head swaying to whatever he was listening to. The snow cut horizontally across the sky, and Marianne fired her shotgun into the field, hoping to make Derek turn around. She couldn't feel her legs, and she was beginning to wonder if she'd make it the last few hundred yards to the car.

Derek didn't hear the shot, and Marianne felt as if she could have pointed the next one his way. But she lowered her head and tottered on until she was grabbing at the door latch.

Derek leapt behind the wheel, his face suddenly white. "What the hell?" he gasped.

"Turn on the heater," Marianne said, her teeth clenched. She was down in the front seat already, stripping her clothes off, a puddle forming at her feet.

Derek switched the blower to high, then jumped out to the trunk and pulled a sleeping bag from Marianne's pack. When she was in nothing but her underwear, he draped it around her. She bent under the dashboard and formed a tunnel for the heat to enter the bag. Then she dropped her head back onto the head-rest and closed her eyes.

"What in the world?" Derek asked. "Did you fall in?"

"There's another one down. It floated across the river."

"Another one?"

"There's two back there. In the ditch. We'll pick them up on the way."

Derek just stared until Marianne peeked an eye open and looked back. She tried to smile, her teeth chattering. "I got three geese," she said, "with two shots. A world record."

"What the hell did you do? Swim for them?"

"Just about. Let's go pick them up."

Derek muscled the car through a turn, and Marianne had to sit up to look for the geese in the ditch. "There," she said, and Derek stopped the car and ran around the hood. When he stooped down and saw the birds, he glanced through the snow to Marianne. He dropped them in the trunk, and when he got back into the car Marianne said, "We'll stop on the bridge and glass for the other."

"What did you do to those birds, Marianne?" Derek asked. "Did you shoot them at all, or just bludgeon them with the gun stock?"

Marianne shivered, remembering the chaotic blows of the wings, the water flying at her from all directions, trying to drag her under. "They tried to kill me," she whispered.

"Looks like it was a close call." Derek fingered her cheek and she flinched. "I think you're going to have a shiner."

Marianne covered her cheek with her hand, and Derek whistled at the scratches across her wrist. "This was supposed to be a side show, Marianne. Not a fight to the death."

"I can't go deer hunting, Derek. I'm soaked."

"Yeah, and deer are a lot bigger," Derek said, shaking his head. "They'd kick your ass."

They drove to the bridge then, and Marianne told him what had happened, and Derek began to laugh, harder and harder. She left out the last of it, of covering the goose with her body until she could hammer it to death.

When they reached the bridge, Derek picked out the other goose before Marianne had even sat up, its white belly stark against the black water. "It's stuck on the shore," he said and drove on. He parked opposite the goose and said, "Don't bother, I'll get it," still joking. "Is it dead?" he asked. "Or is this some kind of trap?"

"I'd take a gun if I were you," Marianne answered, though she didn't much feel like joking.

When Derek retrieved the final goose and put it in the trunk, he slipped back behind the wheel and said, "Didn't even have to get wet."

Marianne kept her eyes closed and she didn't smile. She pretended she was asleep, and she felt Derek turn the car once more, headed for home. It wasn't funny, she thought, not something to be laughed over. She'd been scared, but now, safe under the sleeping bag, the heater roaring hot enough to burn, her feeling began to return, and what she felt more than anything else was the life beneath her fingers when she'd grabbed the necks, the grim determination of the geese to live, even if they had to beat her or drown her to do it. Her own determination had flared against that, but now she was not sure she could point another gun so easily after another bird.

She recalled the long, painstaking stalk, the total shock of the geese when she'd appeared beside them on the cutbank, and her feeling of victory at that moment, even at the moment the three geese lay in the black water, apparently dead.

But something had snapped in her as she beat the goose with the rock. It wasn't a game anymore. Though she knew it wasn't anything so dramatic, soaked and out of breath on the beach, her clothes like icy lead, she had felt as if it was kill or be killed. She'd gone beyond hunting into violence, a violence that was just now beginning to scare her, and she wondered if the hammering beat of the geese in her hands hadn't pushed her out of something as tangled as the thicket, hadn't allowed her to see through to an opening of a different sort.

Out of the blue Derek said, "Tomorrow it's deer. And I'm going to make sure your shotgun stays home."

Marianne kept her eyes closed, and she wondered if that would be any different, seeing the deer so clearly magnified through the scope, knowing exactly where the bullet would hit and what it would do. That was nothing like birds, which were only blurs at the end of a crisp line of barrel. Even when she knew she'd shot well, she'd always have to look, to see how much the shot had done.

She peeked over at Derek and whispered, "Deer will be fine." Then she closed her eyes again and pictured the high, windswept grasses, where one shot could always end a season, just like that.

The Spartan Way

As we rattled down the northwoods highway, the trees so thick and tight to the shoulders it felt more tunnel than road, our driver let us know he was soon quitting his job to return to college. He was majoring in nothing, he said, and as he watched empty-handed while we unloaded our gear and carried it over the first portage to the lake, it seemed a skill he'd mastered without need of further training.

He prattled cheerfully as we packed our two canoes. Paul and I tied everything down whitewater style, and he asked if we were planning on tipping over. Sheena and Mary giggled, and I tugged harder on the tiedown. I was used to whitewater, not still, but habit is habit and it couldn't hurt. As I tied in the food pack, twice as heavy as I remembered, I said, "What the hell happened to this thing?" No one answered, though Mary and Sheena moved away from me, whispering.

A quarter of a mile later, alone at last on the water, we pulled out for another portage. The visitor center film in Ely had gone on endlessly about Le Grand Portage, and every time we had to carry our canoes over another stretch of land, Sheena would ask, "Is this Le Grand Portage?" She tried to imitate the French accent of the film, but came out sounding more like Pepe le Pew. Every time I'd collapse with the food pack, I'd say that this might just be it. I couldn't get over its newfound weight.

It took two or three of those portages before I began to skimp on the tiedowns, and five or six before I gave them up completely. Sheena giggled when she noticed.

I'd had my own giggle the night before, when the outfitter gave the astute wilderness tip of looking at the bend of submerged weeds to determine stream direction. "If you should get yourself all turned around fighting some trophy walleye," he'd explained. I must've looked impressed, and encouraged, he went on. "Now that'll only work on the rivers, not the lakes. And make sure they're all the way underwater, so the wind don't mess you up."

I guess I remembered how different the rivers in the Boundary Waters could be from those I knew in Montana, though it'd been fifteen years since I'd put a canoe in here. But when my brother and his wife wrote from New York suggesting a week-long trip up here, I'd taken over all the planning. As an old river guide myself, who better qualified?

I'd written the Ely Chamber of Commerce for information and within two weeks had thirty-two outfitter brochures—every one from the best and oldest in the land. I'd picked the guide that promised the least-traveled routes. He said, flat out, that he understood the user's need for solitude.

I'd added up the prices and called my brother, saying it'd be cheap, only about fifty bucks for the canoe rental and half that for the shuttle. I told him I'd bring my own canoe and everything else we'd need, and we laughed at all the offers for total outfitting—food, clothes, guides, supplies, everything with a price tag to match. I accepted my brother's praise for getting all that tedious background work done so quickly and so well. We were both pleased to be going the old way. The Spartan way.

But last night in the outfitter's cabin, after he'd gotten the wilderness tips out of the way, the old boy began pulling out the fine print and hidden expenses, using party to mean group here, individual there. The shuttle was twenty-four dollars per party. He'd meant individual there. He knew I'd traveled a thousand miles east and my brother a thousand miles west, and he knew we were stuck. By the time we got through that skinning, we had a two hundred and fifty dollar hole in our hides. As we walked out, my legs a little shaky, Paul sidled up close and whispered, "Yup, yup, it's gonna be cheap. Fifty bucks, maybe a hair more."

Then, during the ride in the crumbling van, Paul had chatted with the driver, asking how busy they were, and the driver had said, innocently enough, that they only had three groups today, and that the old boy had put them all in at the same place, making everything easier. "They're *all* going in here, making the same trip?" I blurted. He nodded happily and said, "Yeah, we already got the Boy Scouts started. They put in a few miles downriver, but it takes those big groups forever to get going. You should catch up to them in no time."

After that I didn't much listen to the driver's drivel. All I could picture was how dry and dusty those outfitter cabins were—how they'd go up at the drop of a match.

As we paddled on alone, Paul and Mary in one canoe, Sheena and I in the other, Paul asked for paddling tips and wondered what kind of lure I thought he should be trolling behind the canoe. He and Mary were both engineers in New York and I should've been giving them a hand, but I was envisioning a night fire, the four of us floating safely offshore in our canoes while the flames plied their way to the stars, a shower of sparks arcing into the sky and hissing onto the water when the outfitter's billboard collapsed. Like fireworks.

At yet another portage Paul finally got my attention, and he put on a Mepps and I a chipped old Daredevil. We towed them behind us as we paddled, and Paul got the first strike, shouting, "Hey, I got one!" and laughing just like a kid. We let the canoes drift as he reeled in, and I shouted useless advice like, "Ease the drag. Keep your rod tip up. No slack. Stay out of the weeds."

Sheena said, "He's doing fine."

Somehow he kept it out of the lily pads and I handed him the net and he scooped up a sixteen-inch northern. His grin split his face, and he whistled, "Check that out!"

I said it was just a baby and told him to throw it back. Even as kids, when we lived in Wisconsin, Paul hadn't been much interested in fishing.

"Are you serious? This is the biggest fish I've ever caught."

"It's a snake," I said. "A youngster." I watched him dip the net uncertainly into the lake. "We'll start saving them for dinner when we get into the real grumpy lunkers."

"I've gone fishing with him forever, you guys," Sheena said. "He's the grumpiest lunker that's ever been in this boat."

I eyed Sheena and she said, "Your turn to catch one, oh guide of guides."

Once we built up speed again, we cast out and hadn't left the bank of lily pads before I had one on, my drag whistling while I tried to drop the paddle and pick up my rod. This was a real fish, and I fought him long enough that we were all curious to see what kind of denizen would be on the end of the line.

When I got it close, the fish's great, flat head bulged the water like some sinister alligator, and we all began whispering without knowing it.

The fish took a turn near the bow of the boat, and Sheena snagged it with the net before I even knew she had it in the water. She got it headfirst, just like you're supposed to, but the next thing she said was, "Jeez, it doesn't even fit."

"Lift it! Lift it!" I shouted, finally not whispering, but the net was a long-handled one, the leverage all wrong, and Sheena couldn't get the fish clear of the water.

"Lift, schmift!" she shouted back.

The pike's predicament finally wound through its prehistoric brain, and all hell began to break loose in that net. I shouted, "Sheena! In the boat! Please!" and the fish thrashed and splashed, and Paul and Mary drew their canoe up beside ours, and over everything I heard Sheena grunt as she heaved, landing the fish in the center of the canoe.

The net folded like an accordion on the hard top of the overstuffed food pack, somehow not sticking to fin or hook, leaving the three-foot-long pike naked as a centerfold. I shouted, "No!" and it gave one great, arcing heave, the Daredevil clearing its mouth and sailing free into the lily pads.

I shouted something else, something unpleasant, but the next thing I heard was the hollow clang of aluminum as the pike touched down at Paul's feet. Suddenly Paul was scrambling back, perching himself precariously atop his seat, crying, "It's got teeth!"

Mary twisted around to see if her newlywed husband was losing vital parts to a panicked fish. It was hard to hear over the drumlike pounding of the pike, but Paul was shouting, "What do you want me to do?" and I was shouting, "Kill it! Before it kills you!"

He shouted, "How the hell am I supposed to do that?" and I shouted, "I don't know."

But the fish took a break, trying to breathe the air for a second, and Paul pinned it to the hull, crying, "I got one!" again. I slipped out my knife, reached into their boat, and speared it through the skull. "Just like with frogs in biology," Paul said, having trouble talking through the racing of his breath.

When the fish stopped quivering, Paul held it up and said, "Man, now this is the biggest fish I ever caught in my life. This is the biggest fish I've ever even seen!"

Before I could say a thing, Sheena said, "Didn't even need a pole. How's that for Spartan?" and Paul slipped a stringer through its gills and tied it to the side of his canoe.

Sheena looked at me. "I thought you were supposed to be the expert?"

Mary snapped a picture of Paul holding up the fish, and then of me doing the same, Paul saying I'd get mad if I didn't at least get to have my picture taken with a fish.

As we paddled on, catching and releasing a pike now and then, nothing like the monster, Paul asked about scaling and filleting, tasks he foggily remembered from high school camping trips. Pretty soon I was back in the guide role, until Mary asked about the night's complete menu, giving a glance at Sheena I should have noticed.

"Menu?" Sheena said. "Didn't you see the way he packed the food? 'Bag a rice, bag a oatmeal. 'Sall you need. We'll catch our food.'"

I rolled my eyes. "I'm not that bad," I said, but they didn't seem convinced.

"It's just the way we used to go," I said. "The Spartan way." I looked at Sheena and Mary and added, "Before either of you were in the picture," thinking I was scoring big. But I heard Sheena whisper to Mary, "Spartan, schmartan. Thank God we went to the store."

It was midafternoon before we ran into the Boy Scouts, their five silver canoes glinting obscenely, jammed into the takeout for yet another portage. I passed the takeout and eyed the little rapid the portage sidestepped. Sheena said, "What do you think, Captain?"

I said, "We can make that no problem," and she said, "Aye aye."

I called out to Paul to hang right and follow the **V** and we'd run it. He yelled "Geronimo!" his boat still in water so flat it'd embarrass a beaver pond. The Boy Scouts scrambled around the rocks shouting, "They're gonna go for it!" and "Watch this!"

I heard the scout leader say, "What they're doing is foolish, boys," and maybe Paul heard him too. We hadn't quite started our run when the same voice said, "Been having any luck fishing?" The voice was full of the knowing pride of a successful fisherman, not unlike a poker player holding all the cards, and I said something like, "Some." I hate talking to other fishermen.

I heard a clink of chain and glanced over just before Sheena and I entered the slip of fast water. The scout leader held up a dripping stringer with two twelve-inch pike dangling from the huge clips. I smiled and turned to my paddling. But the rapid really was nothing much, and even as I did a little draw I could hear Paul call, "Check this out."

I couldn't turn around just then, but I heard the clamor of scout voices wanting to know where, on what, what size, how deep, and all the rest. Paul must've been just at the top of the first rapid he'd run in fifteen years when he called back, "It jumped into the boat!"

A moment later Paul popped out the other side of the rapid, where the river once again gave away its direction only by the bend of weeds. He never said if his grin was from the burst of speed or the look on the scoutmaster's face.

That evening, after a long uphill portage to a private little lake the outfitter had secretly recommended to us, I got everybody started on squaring away camp. While Paul set up a tent, Mary filled a bucket for the rice and tea and dish washing. As she carried it to the fire ring, she said, "Gross! What's this?"

She sounded disgusted enough to investigate, and we all crowded around her bucket. She'd inadvertently trapped a long, greenish gray leech, which now swam around the edge of the bucket, oozing between fat and thin as it undulated along.

"It's a leech," Paul said.

"Like the bloodsucking kind?"

"What's the Spartan menu for gourmet leech?" Sheena asked.

"Sick!" Mary said. "Looks like a piece of live liver."

I told them to leave it there and I'd use it for bait later on. "Walleyes love them," I said. "And we love walleyes."

We left the bucket to begin gathering firewood, when we heard the empty bonging of the Boy Scout canoes at the end of the portage. I swore some more about the outfitter, and Sheena asked me why I didn't leave the rest of the setup to them and go fishing for a while. I looked at her and she nodded, saying, "And take your buddy the leech with you, so we can get dinner started."

I took her advice and went out alone, working a little bay for walleyes, when I heard the crash of the other party's canoes at the portage.

I paddled deeper into the weed-choked bay, hiding, and I put on the leech and cast it out to sit on the bottom. Then I lay back on the deck plate, the late sun still warm but golden now, cutting through the tops of the trees, burnishing the flat water of my bay. Once on the water the strangers' canoes were silent and I was able to forget them.

A family of loons was working the entrance to the bay, and they'd give their warbling cry now and then. I shut my eyes and smiled, not having heard that for so long. The canoe drifted with a breeze, and I let her go where she wanted.

When I guessed it was time to get back to camp, I reeled in my line to find that I'd drifted over it and the leech had taken the opportunity to attach himself to my canoe. I had to scrape him off with a knife. I released him then, watching him swim away as eerily graceful as he'd been circling in the bucket, the hook seeming to have caused no damage at all.

I chased the loons a little way back toward camp, the chicks crawling onto their mother's back and sliding off. Once she dove and they bobbed on the surface a second before following her down. I hadn't seen a loon in a long, long time, and before today Sheena had never heard one. I started to paddle harder to get back to our camp.

When I left the last of the bays, I saw Sheena and Paul and Mary stretched out on the granite that dropped from our camp to the water, soaking up the last of the sun. Smoke from their fire drifted up behind them. Sheena called out something, loud over the water but unintelligible with the distance. I waved my paddle and she called again, and this time I could make out what I thought was, "Get your ass in for happy hour."

I paddled even harder, and when I beached my canoe, they were all smiling. I asked what was up, but they just lifted their plastic cups to me in a toast. "Take a break, Spartacus," Sheena said, holding out my battered and blackened tin coffee cup.

I sat cross-legged on the gray stone with them, and from behind her back Mary pulled out a cardboard box of wine, the five-liter kind with a spigot. She asked, "Would you prefer white?" and Sheena continued, "Or red?" pulling out another box.

I thought of the back-breaking weight of the food pack, somehow my responsibility on all the portages. "White," I murmured, and Paul handed me a cracker covered with some kind of whitish paste. "Good choice," he said. "Goes better with Brie."

After Mary filled my cup from the spigot, Sheena lifted her glass and said, "Cheers."

I sat staring at my wine and cheese. "Cheers," Sheena repeated.

I lifted my cup slowly and said, "Here's looking up your old addresses."

"Now that he knows what he's been carrying through all

those portages, they're really going to be Le Grand Portages," Mary said.

"Le Grand Portages de Grumpy Lunker," Sheena added, again sounding like Pepe le Pew.

I held my glass out to Mary for a refill, and from where I sat it was impossible to see any of the other canoes or camps. The smoke from our fire wreathed around our happy hour, and Mary filled my glass and passed it to Sheena, who handed it to me. I leaned back against the food pack, snuggling in until I was perfectly comfortable.

"You know," I said, "this is exactly how it'll feel when that outfitter burns down," and we all raised our glasses again.

Heads

CARLTON SAT DUCKED DOWN IN THE SAGE, shivering and peering through the thin branches of a ragged little pine, the only tree he could see between the river and the mountains. He told himself he couldn't possibly be cold. It wasn't that cold out. If he was still shivering this hard when the outfitter came to take him back to the lodge, what in the world would they think of him?

He set his rifle in the crook of one of the spindly pine's branches. When he was sure the tree could support the weight, he let go and hugged himself, rubbing his hands up and down his arms. He still kept staring up at the mountains, the mountains the sun had set behind what seemed like hours ago. But he no longer felt the tingling run of anticipation he had when he'd stepped out of the Land Rover. He'd even been whispering then, though the guide smiled and shouted, "Good luck," before roaring off.

The guide had had the heat on in the truck, and now Carlton had a chill he couldn't shake. He wished he'd thought to bring a thermos. But the outfitter had a way of talking that

Carlton smiled at now. He'd had Carlton worked up so much he'd really expected to come out here, hide in the sage for a minute or two, then shoot some sort of world record elk.

It was nearly dusk now, and Carlton decided he'd never sat in a place more distinctly unelkish. Except for the mountains, launching out of the plains like some great wall, there was nothing before him but the huge flats of sage. Behind him was the river, thick with cottonwood and spruce and fir. In there he could at least believe in the elk. He could sit tight in the deep, dark, thick stuff, imagining each twig snap, each gingerly step of a huge bull.

But the outfitter had said they pour out of the hills to the river in the evening. He'd patted Carlton's back and said with an eye like his and a rifle like his, he'd put Carlton way out in the open, where he could take his pick at hundreds and hundreds of yards. "There's one little tree they seem to steer by. It's a sure bet. Just sit tight and let them come to you," he'd advised. "Plenty of time to pick exactly the one you want on your wall." Carlton had felt good about that and had proudly taken his stand at what the outfitter called the gutting tree.

That all seemed like half a lifetime ago now. Carlton sat alone, hugging himself for warmth, straining to hear the sound of the Land Rover crawling up the old river terraces to retrieve him. The river was all he could hear, though: the soughing of the wind through the cottonwoods, the occasional rumble of what must be a leaping rapid, a rush of noise occasionally rising to a crescendo that reached across the sage. Carlton pictured a strainer, a leaning tree caught in the water, bouncing free at slow, regular intervals only to be sucked immediately back under. The water would be freezing.

For quite some time Carlton had picked up another sound, which seemed to come from the other direction, even from the sage itself. Odd scraps of some sort of chuckling, questioning murmurs. At first he'd guessed coyotes, then maybe sage grouse or some kind of bird like that. But as the dusk began to wrap around him, he began to put his money on imagination. In the woods at night he'd heard whole legions of imaginary creatures.

So Carlton sat and waited for the truck, hugging himself, deciding he'd insist on the riverbottom tomorrow. He'd like the mountains themselves, like to test his legs on their steepness, but they were closed into the refuge. He raised his eyes to them but found that the mountains had grown difficult to look at, seeming to glow around their edges as the sun sank and the gloom deepened.

Carlton looked back down at the sage where he'd expected the big bulls to somehow materialize, and now it too seemed to glow, nearly to pulse with some sort of evening aura. The odd babble was louder for a moment, as a breeze curled into Carlton's face, carrying the sound.

Carlton still had no idea what could be making that noise, but he picked up his rifle, feeling better holding it while the mysterious sounds eddied around him. He shivered, spooked, thinking he'd been reading far too much Stephen King. He closed his eyes, hoping they'd adjust to the gloom, telling himself not to look at the bright horizon again. He felt his rifle, cold and heavy in his hands, and he listened to the babble, almost able to distinguish individual voices. He wondered if he could possibly be hypothermic, if his brain might not be turning to ice.

When he opened his eyes, he was looking down, straight at the crisp, clean lines of the Weatherby in his hands. His breath, which had begun to speed up, eased. He lifted the rifle to his shoulder and put his cheek against the stock. There was still barely enough light to see through the scope, and Carlton swung it across the top of the sage, embarrassed he'd let a sound he'd made up get under his skin like that.

For a moment he thought they were the tops of trees, dead

aspen maybe, a drowned stand of branching gray limbs. But he had studied the area so long in full light he knew there was no such thing out there.

They were antlers. Moving, dipping, bobbing antlers. An entire murky horizon of them. Carlton clicked off his safety, though as yet he couldn't even see a head. Nothing but racks.

As soon as he saw the antlers, Carlton understood what the sound was. He'd never heard it before, but he knew instantly that it was the voice of the herd. The sounds seemed to leap at him, and Carlton closed his eyes again, even rubbed at them for a moment, but when he opened them the antlers and the voices were still there.

Soon there were ears, then complete heads, and necks, and, more gradually, the full, heavy bodies of elk. The herd was still a few hundred yards off, milling and whispering, coming on slowly all the time. For a moment Carlton started to count, but then he just watched through his scope. There were hundreds—more than he could possibly count.

Carlton lowered his rifle, suddenly wondering if any of this was real. The top of the sage still glowed with its murky light, the antlers fading in and out of the gloom. It was too dark for a shot, Carlton knew, and even if he could see he couldn't shoot into the middle of a herd like that.

A new bout of shivering attacked him, and he quaked, the hair on the back of his neck standing up. The guttural barkings of the elk surrounded him now as tightly as the night. The elk were closer, probably not a hundred yards off, and he could pick out cows and the shorter shapes of the calves. Would they all be bunched up like that, he wondered? The season was late, the rut gone, but he wasn't sure if real elk would gather together.

Suddenly there was one short, harsh bark and silence. The herd was no longer moving. Each rack stood etched against the fading skyline, all pointing to the south, where the Land Rover had disappeared so long ago. Carlton turned that way too, thought he could hear the rumble of the engine, even the grind of river rock beneath the wheels. Then a new, closer rumble filled his ears. The thunder of the elk's stampede resonated through his body, sounding deep within his lungs. When he turned, the herd was gone. The rumble of their retreat lasted a few seconds more, and then Carlton was alone again behind his little pine.

A pale, white wash stained the southern sky for a moment, and Carlton knew the Land Rover had crested the last river terrace, its lights sweeping the sky. His skin tingled with a run of goose bumps, and he pulled the bolt on his rifle to take the shell out of the chamber. He didn't have any idea what he'd tell the guide.

His knees were stiff when he stood, caught in the Land Rover's headlights. He shrugged, holding up empty hands, and crossed the two-track in front of the truck's ticking grill. He opened the back door and locked his rifle into its hard case before sitting down in front with the guide. He didn't close his door right away, and the guide asked, "Well?"

Carlton looked over at him and shivered. "Do you have a flashlight?" he asked. "I thought I saw something. I'd like to check for tracks."

The guide dug out a big electric lantern, and together they walked out into the dark sage, the silence so tight around the lantern's circle it seemed to ring. "Did you take a shot?" the guide asked. "Are we looking for blood?"

"No. Just tracks."

"Elk?"

Carlton whispered, "Yes," his eyes never leaving the ground. They walked past the gutting tree, and soon Carlton said, "They should be right around here."

But there were no tracks. They looked for maybe a minute

before the guide said, "Sometimes it gets hard to tell in the dusk just what you're seeing."

"I know that," Carlton said. Then he let out a quick rush of breath. "There," he said, too loudly. "There."

Just at the edge of the lantern's ring of light, the dusty, dry soil among the sage was broken. They stepped forward until they stood in the middle of a torn path, the sharp smell of broken sage rising up to sting their nostrils.

"Holy shit," the guide whispered. "Did they come after dark?"

Carlton nodded, and they started to walk north in the churned-up dirt, then south, the guide continuing to whisper, "Holy shit!" every so often. "How many were there?"

"Hundreds," Carlton whispered.

"I've heard of this," he said. "But I've never seen it."

"I'm glad you can see it," Carlton said. "I was beginning to wonder if I had."

"I bet," the guide said.

He killed the light when they reached the truck, and Carlton said, "The whole sky was full of antlers. Giant, giant racks."

"Couldn't get a shot?"

"No. It was too dark." Carlton was quiet for a moment. "I never even really thought of it. Of shooting." He looked at the guide as the dome light flashed on. "I've always heard of that, of guys so caught up they forget to shoot." Carlton laughed a little. "Always sounded like a load of crap to me. I mean, I thought it was a way to hide a missed shot, or some other blunder. Who could forget to shoot?"

The guide shrugged noncommittally and Carlton fell silent. When they were nearly back at the lodge, Carlton said, "I wasn't even sure they were real. Not until we both saw those tracks."

"I bet," the guide answered again.

They walked to the lodge together, but Carlton said he was

heading up for a hot bath and if they could send up a little something to eat that would be great. He'd started to shiver again, and he did not want to talk about this to anyone. He saw the outfitter glance at the guide and then ask, "Same place in the morning? Or do you want to try sneaking into the bottom?"

"Same place," Carlton said. As he started up the stairs, he heard the guide explain, "The ghost herd damn near swallowed him whole."

Carlton did not sleep that night. When he closed his eyes he was engulfed by towering, branching, black racks. Even with his eyes open in the dark room, the endless chatter of the elk surrounded him, a sound he'd never heard and was now afraid would never leave his head.

When the guide came for him in the morning, Carlton swung the door open at the first hint of a knock, startling another "Holy shit!" out of him. "Scared me," the guide said, grinning in the dim hallway. "Breakfast's ready."

"I'll take something with me. I'd like to get out there early." Carlton had his rifle case in his hand.

"They spooked you, didn't they?" the guide whispered. "Don't worry about it. There's plenty of time. We'll rustle up something to eat and head out."

"I'd like to go now."

"It's darker than the inside of a cow out there now, Mr. Lansford. Snowing too."

"That's OK."

Pretty soon the guide gave up. "Suit yourself," he said, chuckling. Carlton grabbed a roll and a cup of coffee. When the Land Rover's engine heated up, the guide switched the heater blower to high, but Carlton said, "Turn it off."

"It's freezing out here, Mr. Lansford. No need to torture ourselves."

"I don't want another chill," Carlton said, staring through

the wiper blades at the steadily drifting snow, flakes as big as quarters.

"Suit yourself," the guide said again, a little less humorously. He tugged his collar up over his neck, and they drove on in silence.

The brakes screeched when they stopped. "The tree's out there somewhere," the guide said, waving his hand at the blackness beyond Carlton's window.

Carlton stepped out and opened the back door for his rifle. "I'll pick you up at noon?" the guide asked. Carlton nodded, and the guide added, "You don't have to go through with this, Mr. Lansford." He pulled a thermos from beside the seat. "We could have a cup, wait for dawn."

"Thanks," Carlton said, "but I'll see you at noon." He started to close the door, but the guide shouted, "Well, here, take this, anyway." He held up the big flashlight they'd used the night before.

Carlton shook his head. "I'm fine," he said. "It'll be light soon enough."

"Morning'll be late with this storm." The guide leaned over, reaching the light farther toward Carlton.

"Noon," Carlton said, and closed the door.

Carlton stood back far enough so that he wouldn't be run over and waited. The cold stung his cheeks, and he could feel individual bits of snow touch his face in the blackness. The Land Rover sat idling, and Carlton could picture the young guide wondering what to do with this lunatic. He was probably picturing some kind of afternoon search. But after nearly a minute the gears ground together, and the Land Rover eased forward. Carlton watched until he could no longer see even the glare of the lights reflecting off the snow.

Alone now, Carlton couldn't see his hand in front of his face. He tried, moving his hand ever closer, flinching slightly when he touched his nose. He still knew where the road was, and he turned his back to it, then started a slow shuffle, never lifting his feet from the ground. He bumped into and edged around sage after sage until he no longer had any idea which direction he was facing. He stood still, to listen for the river, but the snow seemed to steal even its traces of sound from the night. He bent forward, feeling for a place to sit, and his face brushed the long needles of the little pine. The gutting tree.

Carlton laughed out loud, the sudden noise startling in the blackness. The elk would be coming up from the river, and he sat down and listened, straining his ears until the world hummed around him. He guessed and turned to face what might be the river, the east. He huddled into his coat and waited.

Carlton kept switching his eyes this way and that, until, finally, he saw a lighter edge to the blackness, the east. He laughed again, more quietly this time, and he turned around. He'd had his back to the river. Soon he could make out a layer of snow on his forearms, on his thighs. He would be nearly invisible, he realized, and he smiled. He wasn't a bit cold.

Waiting, Carlton wondered if the elk would leave the dense cover of the river in the middle of the storm. Light began to suffuse the eastern rim of sky, and Carlton flipped back his scope covers and checked the shooting light. Just barely enough. The world was a thick gray, and the snow continued to layer over Carlton.

When the herd appeared this time, humping suddenly over the terrace in front of Carlton, they were not talking. They were moving seriously, with purpose, the snow whitening their backs, blending them into the opposite river shelves until Carlton again wondered if they were real. The sage became a silver-gray trail behind them, the clinging snow knocked clear by their passage.

Carlton held his rifle at the ready, scanning through the cows and calves, which led the way this morning. The antlers behind them broke into the lighter sky across the river, but the bodies were still caught in the mass of the marching herd.

The cows led the herd to the south of Carlton's tree, not fifty yards away. As they passed, he could again hear their mumbling, much quieter than it had been the night before, subdued. Carlton had his rifle up now, the scope turned down as far as it would go, 3X, searching through the massive heads for the single one he would like to stop, to take away with him as a piece of the ghost herd he could see and touch forever.

The snow was deep between the sage, and when the cows got behind Carlton and picked up his scent and began to run for the refuge, he realized that before, when they had been walking, they had made no sound.

The herd stretched out as it ran, galloping more than all-out sprinting, and Carlton held his breath. He had the bulls in his scope, noses turned toward the air, antlers swept down along their backs. As more and more bodies flitted through his scope, Carlton managed to capture an individual bull in his cross hairs, and he swung the rifle with its run.

Carlton swung completely around, until his bull was between him and the mountains, and he'd begun to think he never would get the open shot he needed. Then suddenly the bull ran clear for a moment, starkly silhouetted against the snow-blanketed sage and the steep rise of the mountain's flanks. Carlton pulled the trigger and the shot roared out, tearing a gaping hole through the silence.

The shot jarred Carlton, but he caught the last of the bull's nosed-over dive into the whitened sage. He had no idea how long he'd been holding his breath, but suddenly, as the rest of the herd blasted into its final sprint, his lungs again vibrating with their hoofbeats, Carlton found himself gasping. He sank down in the snow and tried to ease in small breaths, never taking his eyes from the spot in the sage where his bull had disappeared.

Carlton waited a long time, several minutes, studying the last spot he'd seen the bull. He guessed seventy-five yards maximum, and he couldn't quite believe the tough, little sage could hide an animal that large. The rest of the herd had simply vanished in the seconds after the roaring clap of the shot, and Carlton tried to reassemble the minute of their passage. He kept glancing at the shining gray trail through the sage to assure himself anything had actually passed.

Finally Carlton looked down at his gun and worked the bolt. He caught the empty brass and worked another shell into the chamber.

As soon as he stood, wondering what he would do if there was nothing there, Carlton saw the arching tan rib cage of the elk down in the snow. Before it, the rack reached up toward the sky, its points rubbed clean and white as ivory.

Carlton walked forward as the day brightened and the snow fell. He was careful not to brush the sage he passed, not to leave a graygreen trail of his own. Then he stood over the elk, which was motionless.

He stared at it for a long time, stunned silent by the sweeping reach of antler, by the girth of the chest. He reached down and patted its side. It was solid and real and dead. No ghost. Carlton pulled the live shell from his rifle's chamber and carried the rifle back to the tree. Leaning it against the little pine again, he walked back to the elk to begin the work of caping.

He looked up at the mountains as he walked, careless of the snow he knocked from the sage, and he thought of the voices of the elk, of the antlers dancing alone on the horizon, and he wondered why he hadn't forgotten to shoot again this morning.

He knelt down at the elk's head and held his knife in his hand. He knew exactly where in his house the head would go, how he would be able to look at it from any chair in which he sat. But he wondered if seeing it like that, that simply, would ever really bring back the long, frozen wait, the blur of all those animals charging so thickly away, the ripple of muscle he had finally brought down.

The head, eventually, would require dusting—would fade into the background blur of the rest of his things—and for a moment Carlton regretted that there wasn't such a thing as catch-and-release hunting.

But as he started his work with his knife, he could picture nights coming in from the office, chilled a little, sitting down to wait for his home's warmth to soak in. Then he could look at this head, could study the dark forks with their white points, the heavy bulk of neck. And then, as the last traces of the chill gave up, making him shiver, he would have to close his eyes. He would have to look at the head from the darkness, the way he had last night, not even sure if it was real, to see it at all the way he had just now, the instant before he had remembered to shoot.

Mountain Boys Fishing Club

DANIEL SNUCK OUT OF THE LODGE long before anyone was awake, even before the kitchen staff had stirred. He stood quietly by his rented car and stared for a moment at the stars, a single band of which he knew was called the Milky Way, but which he had never before seen and alone far outstripped the number of stars he had known to exist. He turned the key far enough to unlock the steering and let the car roll down to the gravel road that led away from the log buildings. He started the engine then and began the drive toward the river.

The mountains around him blocked the stars, and here and there Daniel could see ghostly silver patches of snow that hung on even now, in September. His guide had said they should be getting new snow at any time. Daniel believed that, even though it had nearly touched seventy the day before. The air had the chill that brought snow. Until yesterday he had never seen a mountain, but he was from Chicago and he knew about snow.

Daniel drove until he was well past the spot they'd put the boats in the day before. He hoped they would work the same stretch of river and not find his car or try to look for him today. He pulled a little way off the road and smelled the sage hot against the engine. During the long nights in his new-smelling apartment in Chicago, poring over the glossy magazines the men at the office had given him, with the pictures of the mountains and the trout and the middle-aged men smiling and catching them, Daniel had known this was a place to be alone in. In Chicago, alone was something else altogether.

Daniel stood in the sage and waited for enough light to walk to the river. It was something that they'd been able to talk him into coming out. The men in the office, the Mountain Boys Fishing Club they called themselves, the M.B.F.C., had been making similar trips for years. Daniel was sorry that the whole time he had been married he had secretly called them the Miserable Bastards Fleeing Chicago. They were an all right bunch, really, if you liked group things, which he never had before. But their divorces had come earlier than Daniel's, and they knew some things about being alone. Daniel was glad they'd taken the time to cajole him into this trip.

But Daniel was anxious to try being alone without being afraid of it, and as soon as a strip of gray in the east lit enough of the woods for Daniel to walk, he headed for the river. He had been listening to the water since he'd shut off the engine, and as the invisible branches touched his face and the dew wet his wading boots, he pictured the rocks in the stream that gave the brightly clear water voice.

He held the rod with the long end behind him, which seemed backwards, but that was how the guide had carried it the day before. He hadn't known a thing about fishing, but he had liked what he'd learned yesterday. He was surprised to find that he had the right kind of rod. He hadn't even known it was a fly rod when he bought it. Originally it had been a present to his son, who at six years old had somehow decided he wanted to go fishing. Daniel remembered coming home with the ridiculously long rod and the way his wife had shaken her head and his son had looked at the rod not knowing what to do with it. The next day she brought home a tiny little pole with a shark for a reel. Pressing down on the menacing fin released the line, and his son had taken it out and fished in the front yard.

They had left the same year, before his son turned seven, and when the M.B.F.C. had convinced him to become its newest member, Daniel had gone into his closet of old things to retrieve the fly rod. Then he had thought he'd never had a more pathetic day, but now, standing on the bank of the shrouded river, he doubted it was really so bad.

He knew nothing about bugs, a subject the guide had explained in such detail he'd convinced Daniel it would be impossible to ever know about them. So he left on the fly they had used the day before but did not detach it from its place near the rod's reel. He stepped into the river, holding the rod forward now but looking down to where the water sliced around his boots and then up the calves of his waders. He could feel the cold even through the neoprene. It felt as good as it had the day before, but suddenly Daniel wished there had been a place to buy coffee. There was nothing like that out here, though, nothing but the lodge, which was behind him now.

Daniel walked until the pressure of the water made him put one leg back as a brace, and then he stood still, with the water pushing against him just above the knee. His breath smoked out but did not blow away. The little clouds of his breathing disappeared into thin air, each one gone before the next one escaped. He tried to blow smoke rings, but his breath was not substantial enough for even that.

The mist on the river was already beginning to break, bits of it swirling by his legs, carried, it seemed, by current rather than any breeze. Daniel wondered if the flow of the water was enough to create its own wind.

The sun was not over the mountains yet, but the valley had

lightened to full day before Daniel made his first cast. The mist was nearly gone by then, and the river looked more like a river than something soft and strong with its own winds and voices. His cast was a cripple, and on his second he tried for more power, but he snagged the bushes on the shore behind him, and he walked out of the river to retrieve it.

When Daniel returned to the water, he tried to remember all the guide had said about casting. Without letting out any line, he waved the rod back and forth, from eleven o'clock to one o'clock. When he tried it with the line out, he heard a sharp crack, and from yesterday he knew he had snapped off the fly. He turned around patiently and walked back to shore, where he sat down and started tying on a new fly. That knot he remembered. It was the one thing he'd had plenty of practice with yesterday.

Instead of rushing into the river again, Daniel lay propped up on his elbows and watched the sun ease down the mountains before him, touch the tops of the tall, dark trees across the river, and more slowly slip down their lengths and touch the water. It was nearly a sensuous advance, bold, for everyone to see, but somehow stealthy too. It reminded him of something his wife used to do. He turned his head away then, and the sun touched the river and changed everything there. The new, sparkling mix of sun and water was so bright it was painful. When the sun reached Daniel, warm already and soothing, he lay down completely and closed his eyes.

When he awoke, Daniel started, surprised and scared to find that he was alone. There was a breeze now, eddying quietly through the spruce, and Daniel had to remember that his wife was not here. Neither was his son. They had never been here. He blew out a long breath and listened to the hissing, whispering mumbles of the trees and river.

He was stiff from the ground and from sleep, and he rolled

toward the river and splashed some of its water into his face. He smiled. It was what Mountain Boys were undoubtedly supposed to do.

There were fish rising in the river now, one from just behind the stump across the channel and another that looked to be right in the middle of the fast water. Daniel watched the quick rings, saw them swept away as soon as they were made. He watched the fish feed for quite a while before he stood and moved out to them.

To his surprise, Daniel's cast landed directly in front of the stump and was pulled around to the exact place the fish had been rising. The current pulled it under there, but Daniel left it in the water, hoping the fish might hit anyway. He was the only one who had not caught a fish yesterday, and as friendly as it had been, he did not want to go back to the lodge and go through the ribbing again, while they all drank scotch and laughed loudly waiting for the call to dinner.

No fish did hit, though, and when his line was cutting a V downstream of where he stood, Daniel pulled it out and cast again. He was far enough from shore this time that he didn't worry about the bushes, but occasionally he would hear the slap of his fly against the water behind him. He laughed at that, but he was all attention when the cast happened to land close to the fish, though nothing came after it before he lost that fly too.

Daniel stayed in the water to tie on a new fly. He wasn't sure if it was the same as the guide had used the day before—they all looked pretty much the same. But then, in the late afternoon, there had been swarms of bugs, patches of them so thick Daniel had ducked when the boat drifted through them. Now Daniel could not see any bugs, and he wasn't even sure if the rising fish were eating. He didn't know what else they'd be doing, but he didn't know anything about fish, or bugs. For a moment he wondered what he was doing out here at all.

The fly he tied on was different, smaller and darker, and he had a hard time just threading the line through the eye of the hook. He mussed it with the stuff that was supposed to keep it afloat, though it didn't seem to do such a good job. When he cast it was to nowhere in particular. The two fish he had seen rising had stopped quite a while before. When the fly was dragged under by the flow of water, Daniel was watching the trees across the river. The sun was flat on them now, nearly straight overhead, and the trees were filled with shadows. They no longer reminded him of his wife, but he could still remember the way the bright warmth of the sun had crept down them, and he knew there were things he would be unable to forget.

Daniel looked away from the far bank and back to his fishing. The heavy, yellow line was bowed in the water, the fly long since pulled under. He gave it the first tug back, and something tugged in the other direction. Daniel was too surprised to do much of anything, until he saw the fish dart through the clear water, exposing a bright flash of silver. Then he hauled in hard on the line, leaving the extra to spool sloppily into the current at his feet. He tried to do everything the way the fishing club members did.

The fish was not big, only about six inches, and eventually Daniel was towing it upstream, the fish's head skipping a little on the surface. He netted it as the fishermen had and watched it breathing or gilling or whatever in hard, docile silence.

Daniel held it finally in his hand, through the netting, and cracked it over the head with his new fishing knife. He did not like that, but there were many things he had to learn. Some of the M.B.F.C. guys slipped their fish into their wicker creels without killing them, saying they stayed fresher that way. But the one member Daniel had shared a boat with had said that was more cruel than killing them outright. Others, or so the guide said, never kept a fish but put them back as soon as they had caught them. Daniel liked that idea, but there were some things he still needed to hold, that he needed to be able to stop and look at again and again, just to assure himself they were still there—that they had ever happened at all.

Daniel compared the fly he had used to the cluster of them in the box the guide had provided. He had one that worked, and he wanted to be able to put on the same kind when he lost it. He pulled out two identical flies and stuck them into the sheepskin patch on his vest, then cast again. Nothing happened.

Soon Daniel was imitating the cross-stream cast and the pull of the line, dragging his fly through the water below the surface. He pulled in now and then, as he had the moment before the fish struck. Another fish hit, no bigger than the first. He towed it in and killed it, and put it in the wicker basket with the other. He was smiling now, beginning to look forward to the night in the lodge.

Daniel caught three more fish as the afternoon waned. He had not brought lunch, and it seemed even hunger was right for this place. He had not moved more than twenty feet from the spot where he'd first reached the river, and he did not want to. He wished there was some way he could take this tiny bit of river with him.

He napped once more late that afternoon, and when he awoke he only looked for his wife for an instant. The clouds of insects were forming again, as they had the evening before, when the guide had said they were getting to the best time to fish.

Daniel stood and without walking into the river made a cast. The surface of the water was dimpled sporadically with small rises, and where the river was flat and gray and glossy with the sun behind the mountains, the bugs leaving the water covered the surface with tiny pockings, as if the world's finest mist was falling. As soon as Daniel's fly touched the water, something took it under, and it was not like the little fish he had in his creel. Daniel knew that even before he brought his rod tip up to let the fish know he was there.

Daniel had not hit the fish hard, and he was not prepared for the violence of the response. The line he held between the fingers of his left hand snapped out of his grip, and the reel began to sound like the screech of something in the city. Daniel stared at the line shooting straight away from him, more and more of it going into the water, straight to the channel fork and the fast water out there. The current began to bow the line in the water, and Daniel knew he did not want to let this fish escape.

He grabbed the line that was pulling away from the reel and stopped it dead. Out in the water, a little past the yellow end of his line, he saw the water hump and a fin just begin to break the surface, and then there was nothing pulling his line away from him anymore.

Daniel stripped line in frantically, trying to pretend the fish was coming back to him, but after a few of those pulls he slowed his retrieve. He knew he'd made a mistake, a big one, and he would never see that fish as anything but a bulge in the water, hell-bent away from him.

When he had all his line in a confused tangle around his legs, Daniel pulled the end of it out of the water and studied the leader, which, as he suspected, was flyless and full of the tiny self-tying wind knots the guide had warned him against. They killed the strength of the line, the guide had said, and as soon as they were found they had to be untied or cut out. There had just been too much for him to remember, Daniel thought. But he knew he never would have taken the time or trouble to cut out all those little knots.

Daniel stumbled walking back to shore, still looking out where the fish had last touched the surface. He dropped his rod as he threw his hands out, but he recovered his balance without falling into the water. He could see his rod on the bottom, turning over in the current, swinging on the heavy reel to point downstream. All he had to do was wait and it would come to him, but Daniel suddenly wanted to leave it there underwater and never touch it again, never bring it back to his apartment in Chicago, where putting it away would mean opening that closet again. "My closet of old things," he said out loud. "I surely am one of the Miserable Bastards now."

But when the twig-thin rod tip touched his leg and he felt the tiny contact, even through the neoprene and the incessant nagging of the current, Daniel bent down, soaking his shirt in the water as he reached for the rod. The rod wasn't where it appeared to be, and Daniel smiled at the refraction, running his hand down his leg until he reached where the rod was still touching him. He pulled it out of the water then and carried it to shore.

Wringing out the sleeve of his new Pendleton, Daniel watched the water splatter dark splotches across the dry, white stones. He looked back to the river then, which was all flat, glossy patches in the dying light, and he thought of the fish and wondered at all that was hidden beneath that steely surface. That reminded him of his wife too, and Daniel closed his eyes for a moment, wondering if he would ever really be alone again.

He thought of the fish, stopped short by his ham-handed fist on the line, like a dog jerked off its feet at the end of its leash. There were things that were just instinct, that he did when he saw everything getting away from him. He'd always heard reactions like that were good, and he wondered how he had been so shortchanged. He remembered shouting and shouting, but now could not recall how he had ever thought that would make her stay.

Daniel stood up and turned away from the river, and started through the band of trees toward his car. He was glad he had retrieved the rod. And he was glad he had the little fish to show, even though he would be kidded for their size. That was better than coming back with nothing. He knew that. But he wondered what he would have done if he had actually landed the big fish. "The big one," he said out loud. "The one that got away."

Daniel laughed quietly, crunching over the cottonwood leaves that had already begun to drop. "You should have seen the one that got away." He knew he couldn't even mention that. Couldn't say how it had surprised him, how the suddenness and quickness and resolve had left him standing dumbstruck until he had said, No! and done the one thing guaranteed to fail.

As he cleared the trees and there was only the pungent sage left between him and his car, Daniel tried to believe he would have let the big fish go. Each time he killed the little ones, he had thought of how much better it would have been to release them. With the big one, which he was sure would have been too beautiful to kill, things would have been different. He would have seen what he had to do.

Instead of digging inside his waders for the keys, Daniel turned and looked at the mountains in the west. Without the sun there to give them relief, they were a mere paper cutout of themselves, flat and dark. There were things that reminded him of, too, and he knew he would have killed the big trout.

Without it no one would have believed him. Released, he would have had the thought of it to carry around and be vaguely proud of, but Daniel had begun to learn how treacherous those private inside things were. He had always thought he would carry pieces of his life with him like that, thought they would carry the two of them through old age and maybe even beyond.

He tried again to replicate, in every detail, the three of them walking down the concrete steps of the hospital. His son—his son, by God—three days old and wrapped tight in the pale, thin arms of his wife. The sun had been shining and his son's eyes were closed, and Daniel had thought, *This is the first time he has ever felt the sun, or the breeze coming down the street.* Even then he'd known he was being maudlin, but he couldn't stop himself. His wife smiled down at their son and only took her eyes away from him long enough to keep from tripping down the steps. He held her elbow, offering what he could. The breeze blew her hair across her face, but she seemed not to notice, and Daniel brushed it back from her eyes. She had glanced at him then, and she just kept smiling. He had loved her so much then that he was sure everything they ever did would be seared into his memory forever.

But already, without them, there was haze creeping into those pictures, and Daniel sometimes wondered if that wasn't for the best.

Daniel unlocked his car and three-cornered it on the empty road and headed back for the lodge. He'd taken his rod down and put it carefully in the trunk. If he had left it in the river, he realized, he would have gone back and searched for it before he left this place. He took the creel with him into the car, and as he drove he lifted the lid and stole glances in at the little fish. He had been right—he was glad to have them like this. It wouldn't last, of course, but right now he was glad to have them.

Daniel drove slowly through the hardest part of dusk, when there is not enough light to see but not enough dark for the headlights to cut into. He was looking forward to the hors d'oeuvres and the scotch, and even to the kidding that would go on about the fish and about his disappearance before dawn. But, he thought, maybe they knew enough about that disappearance that they would not mention it. Maybe they even knew enough that they would be reminded of their own early times and not want to bring it up, or even talk to him.

Daniel strained to see the road in front of him, and the visibility kept getting worse. There was a constant pattering sound, as if it were raining, but Daniel knew there was not a cloud in the sky. He turned on his headlights and saw clouds of bugs, reflecting his lights like snow or fog. He turned the lights off and realized the rain he had been hearing for some time was really the tiny bodies of the insects dashing against his car, invisibly smearing his windshield until he could barely see.

Daniel pulled off the road and tried to wipe his windshield clear with a rag, but that only made it worse. He looked out to the dark band of trees that hid the river, but it would be dangerous to go out there for water without any light. Daniel sat against the hood and waited. The guide said the bugs were knocked down by the night's cold, and he waited for that. This was a country he did not know, and he would have to follow the lead of the experts.

He thought once more of the big one, the one that got away, and he was glad he did not have it in his creel. He hoped that if there was a next time he would have the strength to let it go, but he was far from sure of that.

When it was truly dark and the cold was something he could feel moving into the night, Daniel pushed himself off the hood and started running stiffly down the road. He was testing for the bugs he could not see, waiting to feel them against his face or not, to see if it was safe to continue down this road. He did not feel anything, and he ran faster and faster, until he was sure he was running as hard as he possibly could, and still he did not feel the tiny bodies.

He stopped when he could go no farther, and he stood in the middle of the empty road, hands on his knees, panting hoarsely for the thin air of this strange landscape. The mountains were still plain, flat shadows of themselves and Daniel turned slowly and walked on shaky legs back to his car.

The headlights had something to grip on to now and work against, and Daniel followed them back to the lodge. When he parked he could see the lights inside and members of the

M.B.F.C. moving around, drinks in their hands, and though he could hear nothing, he knew they were laughing.

Daniel got out of his car and one by one took the little trout out of his creel and snapped them into the enormous clips of his metal stringer. He wanted to push through the door of the club, into the dazzling warmth and light, and have the fish right there in front of him, and he wanted to feign pride in his ridiculous catch while his eyes were useless, doing everything they could to adjust to the change in light.

By the time he would be able to see his fellow members, their embarrassment and fear of seeing what they once were would be gone, and they would see the fish and know they had something to latch on to to get past the hard part, when the nakedness of the scars was so plain. The fish would bring every-one back to what they were here for, and they would laugh then, just as the room was becoming visible to him, and they would tug at the fish on the stringer and clap him on the back and joke about what a fight they must have put up, and someone would thrust a wide, heavy glass into his hand and he would blame the warmth of the lodge for the redness of his face.

Daniel saw all that clearly as he stringered the last of the fish. He looked up to the sky, at the stars that were visible there now, nearly as strong and bright already as they had been that morn-ing. He walked toward the lodge and reminded himself, in an audible whisper, to say nothing of the one that got away.

Legacy

VAN WONDERED IF he'd ever really been as much a jackass as the man hopping through the sage beside him. He grinned a little, turning away so the other man wouldn't see. Denny considered himself deadly serious. He wouldn't appreciate any grinning.

Stepping around a sage, Denny slowed, then stopped. He stooped over on the dry, dusty hillside. "Tracks," he said. "Tons of them."

Van laughed. "Do you want to follow them?"

Denny glanced quickly at Van. "They're here," he said.

"They're all over. That's what we've been shooting at all day." Van reached into his game pocket and brought out a stiff chukar. He couldn't help himself. He brushed the disheveled feathers and held it out to Denny. "Want to see what one looks like?"

"Up yours." Denny tried hard to smile, and Van knew that wasn't an easy thing when empty shells were all that filled his pockets. Denny started hiking again, uphill, through the black rock and dry sage, putting on speed. He was in shape. Van had to give him credit for that. He fell into the pace a little off to the side.

Halfway up the hill they were puffing hard, and they paused for a moment. Van wiped sweat from his forehead. Denny had stopped talking for the first time all day, and Van felt bad about showing him the chukar. Though they'd sat side by side at work for nearly a year now, they didn't know each other well enough for that kind of joking. He remembered the pictures on Denny's desk and he asked, "How's that kid of yours doing?"

"Good," Denny said. Between breaths he added, "She wanted to come along. She's still too small for a shotgun, though. I tried telling her this was man stuff. That was the wrong thing to say. You should have seen her face. Looked like thunder. Looked just like her mom."

Van smiled and looked over at Denny, never having imagined him trying to talk to his daughter. He wanted to ask what it was like having children, but he doubted they knew each other well enough for the answer to mean anything.

Denny was looking up the hill, and he caught a glimpse of fleeting shadows darting from sage to sage at the same time Van did. "They're running for the crest," he shouted, and he started off after them, lunging up the steep, gnarled ridge. Sweat had turned the neck of his shirt black, and the upper seam of his canvas vest was rimed with a thin, white ring of salt. Van started running too.

The first bird, nearly at the lip of the hill, took off, clearing the sage by a foot, and Van heard Denny's gun boom. The chukar was visible only for the instant it popped over the ridge, and Van wondered if Denny had even been able to see it when he pulled the trigger.

But the shot spooked some of the birds that weren't so far up the hill, and suddenly there were quick targets everywhere. Van picked out the first fleeting shape and swung with it. It crumpled when he fired, and he swung carefully to the next, but they were over the hill before he could shoot.

The last straggler launched out only a few yards ahead of Denny, seeming to know it'd never make the ridge. Instead it turned, leaving Denny's first shot far to the left. Then it set its wings, going back down the hill, gaining speed on the downhill swoop. Denny's second and third shots from the semiauto came one on top of another, before the bird was twenty yards away. The fourth shot didn't come, and when Denny started to swear, Van took the bird.

Momentum carried the dead chukar a long way down the hill. It hit bare dirt with a small puff of dust and bounced, coming to rest in the upper reaches of a gray sage.

The hills were oddly quiet after the rapid bursts of firing. Van opened his over-and-under and pulled out the spent shells. He closed the breech on empty barrels. Denny pumped shell after shell into the magazine of his shotgun. When he started to turn up the hill, Van said, "Your empties."

Denny flashed a scowl but stooped down and kicked through the sage until he found the scattered bright green hulls.

Van let loose a sigh and backtracked down the hill to pick up the fallen bird. His legs were beginning to tire, and he knew he'd have to race to keep Denny from blundering on ahead. He stopped and looked at the dead chukar, almost lifelike in the branches of the sage. Its eye was still open inside the bandit-mask stripe. A bright drop of blood clung to the edge of its beak, but otherwise the bird looked as perfect as ever, as if the shot hadn't hit at all. Van reached down and lifted it carefully from the sage. He smoothed the ruffled feathers and wiped away the drop of blood. He started slowly back up the hill and was surprised to see Denny sitting down holding his other bird, already gutted. Denny held it up and shouted that at least now he knew what they looked like. He laughed.

Van climbed. He rarely took people hunting with him. But Denny had acted like such a pup, even bringing his new

Browning into the office to show off. And Van had always liked the way the pictures of his little girl crowded Denny's desk. His own looked so barren beside that. It was good to see him relax a little. During the day, as the tally grew more and more lopsided, Van had begun to wonder if this hunt wouldn't grow into something that would sit between their desks at work.

Breathing hard and sweating, Van checked for cactus and collapsed into the hard dirt beside Denny. He pulled the water bottle from his vest and took a long swig, some of the hot water sloshing past the corners of his mouth and dribbling onto his chest. He passed the bottle to Denny.

"How many have you got now?" Denny asked.

"Limit."

"Want to turn back?"

"We'll get yours too."

Denny laughed a little. "I'm not sure we've got enough time. Or shells."

"Just slow down a little."

"I can't believe I keep missing. I did all right at the trap club."

Van looked down the series of high ridges to where they petered out into the long flats leading back home to Vegas. The sun, even in the fall, made the flats almost white. They shimmered. "Think of how it'll feel when you bring one down," he whispered. He took another drink from the bottle.

"If."

Van smiled and looked right at Denny. "You know how long I've been doing this?"

"A long time."

"Right."

"But I know I can shoot," Denny said. It sounded whiny, and he looked away, out toward the same flats.

Van remembered times when, like Denny, he'd pulled the

trigger as fast as he could, just because the birds seemed to be vanishing before his eyes. "You're in the frustrating part right now is all," he said. "These aren't clay pigeons. Once you start hitting, you'll be having the most fun you've ever had. That'll last a long, long time."

"How many times have you missed today?" Denny asked.

"A couple."

"Once. I counted. That sounds like fun to me."

"Wait until you hit one. Those misses'll be something sweet then."

Denny didn't answer and Van looked off the dry mountain toward home. "You should've brought your kid up here today," he said.

"And let her see me shoot like this? No thanks."

Van shook his head and stood up, pocketing both the small, warm birds. "Ready?"

"I've gone through more than a box of shells already."

"Shooting's fun. I haven't gone through a box of shells in a day in years."

Van started up the hill, and Denny fell into place twenty yards to his side. They didn't talk again until they reached the top. They looked ahead into the steep, jumbled cut and up the next hot, broken ridge. "Where do you think they went?" Denny asked.

"Probably halfway up the other side. Same as ever." Van peeked over at Denny and smiled. They both knew they were wearing out. "Want to look for tracks?"

Denny laughed out loud. "Up yours," he said. They started down the hill, the sage scraping at their legs and the rocks breaking free and crunching a turn or two down the side. "If we don't kick them up here, we'll start to circle back toward the truck," Denny said.

Van nodded. "It'll be getting dark soon anyway."

By the time they did circle back to the truck, Denny had his first chukars. A pair. A brace he called them. He kept saying they were his first double, and Van didn't say anything. He wondered if a double was a double if it took four shots. He knew there wasn't a question about it as far as Denny was concerned.

When they reached the truck, they tucked their guns into their cases and slipped them behind the seat. They stretched the birds onto what was left of the ice block in the cooler. Van smiled when he saw Denny set his carefully off to one side, as if his two would taste a bit different than any of Van's. Then he guessed his first ever, fed with fanfare to his wife and daughter, probably would taste different.

Van turned the lights on and drove carefully down the impossibly steep, old mining roads. Denny prattled on and on about the two birds he'd hit, about how he'd seen them and for once had picked out a single bird, and how he'd known he'd hit as soon as he pulled the trigger. He asked if Van had seen them fall. And Van had, of course. With his limit he'd been carrying an empty gun and all there was to do was watch.

He'd seen the birds get up unexpectedly, near the top of the ridge again, but unseen before the flush. The sun had been low—fiery—with no clouds reddening the sky. Van had watched the birds disappear toward that, small blurs vanishing into the blinding edge of sky. He'd seen Denny lift and swing, picking out a bird on the purplish fringe of the sunset, and he'd imagined how the blur at the end of the barrel would become a chukar, frozen in midflight at the second he would pull the trigger, almost without realizing he was firing.

Denny had fired three times at the first bird, and Van had thought of old movies—sprays of dirt following the charging soldier until they caught up with him and he folded into the ground. He saw the shots jolt Denny's shoulder, the shells arcing out of the gun into the fading light.

But when Denny had swung on the second of his double, somehow Van had known he had it figured out. That was when the blur had stopped being a blur for Denny, too, and now in the truck, barely listening to the excited chatter, Van knew that Denny would be doing this for a long, long time and that he had started it for him. He didn't much care, and he wondered who he would want to give this to.

Denny, slightly embarrassed now, stopped talking about himself. He switched to the birds he'd watched Van take. He told how the last one had bounced, kicking up a cloud of dust. He marveled at how all Van had to do was raise his gun and it was curtains for another winged creature.

Van knew Denny wanted him to join in, to reciprocate, to tell him all about how his birds had looked. All he could do was glance over and say, "Winged creature?"

Denny stopped talking for a moment. Then he laughed. "Well, Jesus, don't you even get excited anymore?"

"Of course," Van said, then wondered if it was true.

"You don't act like it," Denny said, still laughing. "You act like your dog just died."

Van bounced the truck over a cattle guard and onto the highway. "How old is your little girl?" he asked.

"Kelly? Twelve."

"And she wanted to go with us?"

"She's an awful tomboy. I always wanted a boy. But we decided right off that we could only handle the one."

Van thought of his home and his wife and whatever evil it was that wouldn't let them have children of their own. "Isn't twelve the legal age for a bird license?"

"I think so. But she's a runt. Hardly bigger than a bird herself."

Van thought of swinging on bird after bird after bird. He couldn't remember when it had become so automatic, when the

adrenaline rush had faded, leaving him with only ballistics prob-
lems to solve with each flush. He remembered the slight stir he'd
felt seeing Denny make his first smooth shot, feeling again a part
of that rush of pride and amazement.

"Next time bring her along," Van said, without realizing he
was going to speak. "I'll show her the ropes. She can use my
twenty-gauge and I'll load it way down, take out the sting for
her."

He looked over and Denny was staring at him. Van
shrugged. "Tell her I asked her to come. So she won't feel like
she's horning in on 'man stuff.' Tell her I'd like to show her this."

Denny still didn't say anything, and Van drove with unneces-
sary concentration, finally giving a forced laugh. "Tell her if she
shoots at all like her old man we'll call her Machine Gun Kelly."

Denny laughed then too, saying, "Up yours," one more time.

When the laughter faded, Van asked, "Do you know anything about adoption, Denny? Is it as impossible as they say?"

Denny said he didn't know the first thing about adoption.
Van said he didn't either. He didn't say that simply mentioning it
to his wife made her cry, that not enough time had passed for
that. When Denny asked why he wanted to know, Van shook his
head. He drove carefully, and he began to tell Denny how he had
looked taking his first chukar, with the low sun ruddy against his
face and the shells arcing out, one after another, into the cool
evening of the desert.

Residents

GARY SQUATTED BY HIS CAMPFIRE roasting a partridge wrapped in clay, the way his mother had when they'd come here as a family. He was tempted to break the little oven open so he could have the smell, but he knew that would ruin the cooking. Instead he lay back in the long, dry bunch grass and watched the blue-black of the sky, picking out the first of the planets and stars.

In the early years, while his father had scraped by following the oil booms, they'd spent their summers camped wherever his father was working, living in an old, dark army tent, his mother riding herd on her four children while his father worked the rigs. His mother canned everything then, preparing for winter before spring had hardly started, the heat of her canning fires driving them all from the tent. Gary and his sister would go fishing then, bringing home sagging stringers of trout, never having heard of limits or licenses. What trout they did not eat his mother would can.

Clouds began coming in from the north, and Gary watched them march across the stars. The wind that eddied through the grass and fanned his fire grew colder, carrying the crispness of dried leaves up from the creek bottom, and Gary edged closer to the flames. He wished his wife were with him, and he thought again about breaking open the clay.

Gary wished he could feel the heat of his mother's canning fires right now, and he could nearly taste the spicy sauce of the canned fish. It had been years since he'd even thought of canning a fish. His parents were in Saudi Arabia now, where his father had found the biggest boom of all.

The winters back then, each in a new cramped house, always seemingly colder than the last, were nothing like the summers. Another year as a new kid in school, with hand-me-down clothes. The canned food was an embarrassment then, and Gary remembered how he had begged to have his sandwiches made on store-bought bread.

Gary sat up and turned his back to the north. He guessed the bird was done, and he rolled the small, blackened ball from the fire. He set several sticks onto the coals and stirred them into flame for light. He cracked open the fired clay with a larger stick, and the bird's steam rushed up. Smelling that, he no longer felt guilty that the openness and the dark and the quiet could make him lonely.

Wetting his fingers in his mouth, he made quick little jabs, breaking pieces of clay off the bird. The feathers came off with the clay, and underneath the skin shone in the light from the flames. Gary juggled the small, naked bird until he could hold it without being burned, watching the glistening skin and the sharp, bulging line of breast.

He ate slowly, pulling the delicate meat from the skeleton with his teeth. He cleaned the bones until they glowed in the firelight, and with his knife he separated the wishbone and dropped it into his shirt pocket.

When he broke open the second ball, the smell of bird and grass and sage and hills floated out of the shattered clay once again, lasting as long as it always did, which was never long enough.

Gary sat by the fire until the first flakes of snow flitted by the flames and disappeared. Then he brought his sleeping bag close and climbed into it with his clothes on. He lay with his eyes open, though now with the starlight blotted all he could see were the quick tracers of snow caught in the dying light of the fire.

By morning the snow hadn't amounted to much beside a change in temperature. The thin layer of granular flakes tucked into the matted grass made it seem brighter than it was under the heavy overcast, but the cold nipped at Gary's face and he didn't get out of his bag until he heard the faint honking of faraway geese.

Gary stared for a moment at the stony, gray face of the sky but could pick out none of the migrating geese. He laced up his boots and glanced around his runt of a camp—nothing but a dead fire, a bag, and a pack. He took his shotgun from under his pack and started down for the quiet bay where the creek joined the Missouri. Even if the geese were already on the move, there would almost have to be ducks on the water the way the night had gone.

He crossed the creek on the beaver dam, climbing the cutbank where he'd gathered the clay for the birds, then slinking through the willows and junipers, crouching lower until he reached the big river. When he stood, nothing flushed, and he was alone on the bank of the river, the water ruffled and gray, stretching out empty before him. The wind traveling down the canyon was stronger and colder than it had been in the hills.

Gary stared out at the river, barely whitecapped, and he wondered what Saudi Arabia looked like. Gary pictured sand dunes and camels, but he knew there had to be more to it than that. That would be like saying Montana was all like this, ignoring the blocky chunks of the Rockies in the west and the flat wheat land of the Highline, even the breaks country farther downriver. This country went on and on, and he couldn't picture a place that didn't.

His camp seemed even more alone than the edge of gray-black water, and instead of turning back for coffee or breakfast, Gary hiked the steep, rocky side of the creek until he came over the top and stood at the rim of the long table of grass, sloping up to the mountains with their trees and their deer and sometimes elk.

The snow crunched a little under his feet, and the grass was louder with the cold. Gary held to the edge, where the grass dropped down to the Missouri in sudden black cliffs. Trees rimmed the top of the cliffs, and sometimes blue grouse sheltered in them. But it was truly partridge that Gary was hunting today, and after giving up the diversion of the ducks and the faint hope of grouse, he moved back out into the heart of the windswept grass.

If he could find the Huns, they'd hang tight because of the wind, and it would be easier to get off a shot. It would be no easier to hit them, though. In the wind they maneuvered like swallows, and in the huge, empty open they seemed no bigger than that.

Gary walked with his gun at the ready, but as he crossed through more and more of the empty grass, he eventually dropped his gun to his side. He was cold now, and he wished he had turned back for breakfast. Although he tried to concentrate on the hunting, he kept wondering where he'd find work next, and when.

He stopped and looked hard at the huge blank space of the sweeping grass and added "dog" to the endless list of things they wanted. Wandering around out here, he was as close to finding a job as he was to finding any birds, and he wondered what he was doing. He turned back toward camp.

Sue, his wife, had insisted he come out here to take a break, but it wasn't helping him find a job, and though her job was good enough for a while, if he didn't get one soon it truly was possible they'd be forced to leave Montana.

Gary swore quietly into the cold wind and threw his gun onto his shoulder, holding it by the barrels now, watching nothing but where he put his feet in the new snow and dead grass.

He walked a long way before the partridge blew out of the grass, handfuls at a time. He was too surprised for the first group and didn't have his gun turned around for the second. He fired at the last singles to break out, but they tore wildly away from the wind and his shot. He watched them fly off and marked where they landed, though they didn't spare any distance with the wind at their backs.

They were so fast Gary had barely seen them, just a rush of brownish streaks, low and tight over the undulating field of buff grass. He opened the barrels of his shotgun and dropped in two new shells. The gun closed with a careful, solid click, and he ran his hand along the barrel, erasing a smudge with the ball of his thumb.

The gun's finish was nearly gone on the receiver and on the front edge of the trigger guard, where his hand rubbed when he carried it low. The tang was silver now, too, from the soft part of his hand, between thumb and forefinger.

Gary had only been ten when his father gave him the gun. It was in the flushest year of the Big Basin boom and they'd spent the summer in the east, on the Yellowstone near Sidney. His father had given identical shotguns to Gary's brothers and sister, but they were older, and Gary had had to watch his in the box for two years before he reached what his father ordained as the twelve-gauge age.

That was only fair, though, Gary thought. Now his brothers and sister could only watch theirs in their gun cases, if they watched them at all anymore.

He knew none of their guns had worn as well. His brothers and sister had let themselves be forced out of state, to L.A., Seattle, and Minneapolis. They still flew in most falls, his sister every fall. But a weekend, or even a week, was certainly not the same as living through each of the seasons.

His brother in Seattle had offered him work once. Gary had had his own job then, but the wages were twice what he was making, and in the face of that nothing he said made sense. His brother had become upset finally. "You're worth more than twice what you make, Gar'. They'd see that. You'd move up like a rocket."

Gary couldn't answer and his brother had grown silent, then apologized. Gary shrugged and said, "Somebody's got to keep scouting the hunting spots for you guys." They made themselves laugh, but his brother had added, "Let me know if I can help with anything," and Gary had said he would. Sometimes it was just easier to say those things. But that offer, innocent enough at the time, loomed larger and larger now. Sometimes it seemed it would be so easy to sell their little house in Cascade, get out from under those payments, and move away to a city someplace where he could get a real job that paid real money.

Gary looked up from his gun and gazed across the endless stretch of grass as if he had just awoken. He tried to laugh again the way he and his brother had, at nothing that was funny, and at his first step toward camp, two late birds broke out, lifting out of what looked like bare dirt and whisking low across the plain in front of him. He fired at the first blur, and it jarred in the air and hit the ground and rolled. On the other already, he hurried his shot because everything was moving so fast.

The second bird wavered, struggled, then fell. Gary ran in as fast as he could, reloading on the run. He jumped over the first bird, its ruffled white-gray belly easy to see, and stopped where the second had gone down. He started to circle rapidly and the partridge kicked out, trying to run and fly at the same time, unable to do either.

Gary finished it in a second. If he pressed fast enough, sometimes they would flush. If he gave them a chance, they hid. Then, unless he stepped on them, they would stay to ground, and it was nearly a miracle how something colored with soft gray and chestnut and rust could blend into a patch of dried, golden grass.

Gary sat in the whipping grasses and gutted the birds. He would have liked quiet now, so he could smooth the birds out and remember nothing but how they had come up and how they had fallen and how the others had been streaks he had hardly noticed and not birds at all, because he was concentrating on the shooting.

He tried lying down to get out of the wind, but it was even louder with his head down in the frenzied sawing of the grass, and he covered his ears with his hands. He saw some open streaks of blue in the overcast but knew it wasn't a clearing kind of sign, just gaps between the clouds that would be in and cold for a long time.

He was still looking at the sky when he heard Sue laughing.

Gary sat up quickly as she crossed the last of the land between them, her shotgun at the ready. When she collapsed into the grass beside him, Gary held the pair of Huns out to her, and she took them and held them in her hands. She always said they were her favorite thing in the world. "I thought I heard four shots," she said.

Gary smiled and shrugged. "No teaching today?" he asked.

"The furnace blew. Instant holiday."

"How'd you get in so early?"

"The furnace went last night. I drove down early. I found your camp," she said. "I knew you'd be up here."

"You must have hiked halfway in the dark."

"I know the way."

She put her arm around him, and Gary was about to tell her how he had missed her last night. It would be a story he would tell with an expression of amazement. But then what sounded like a shot cracked out, and they both turned toward the mountains. Before they looked away there was another crack and Gary said, "Bighorn."

They fell in next to each other, moving up the slope toward the broken stretch of ridges leading to the mountains. They smiled when they heard the sounds, but they spread out slowly until they were split the proper distance to put up the Huns without letting them escape between them.

Gary watched her more than the grass where the birds would be. The lonely, repetitive cracks continued to drift down from the mountains. He pictured the bighorns battling up there in the dry, windswept ridges, and he wondered if they fought only for the ewes, or if they fought over the empty land itself. He had seen them before, rearing high and dropping down to stagger back and blink and crash again, and he hoped they fought for the land.

Sue steered straight toward where the bighorns were butting heads, but as they entered the first of the deep gulches, it became harder to give a direction to the crack of the horns. Gary turned uphill and moved quickly, carrying his gun at his side. Sue held the pace, and when they crested the far side of the gulch, they stopped to listen, but now the country folded and climbed and gullied, and the sound, like everything else, surrounded them.

Gary took a guess and charged down into the next cut and up the other side. They were breathing hard when they reached the crest, and they could see the Missouri, so far below, hemmed in by black rock, pewter glimpses through tossing branches of pine. The wind was cold, and it dried their sweat and made them shiver. With the swirls of the wind, the rifle-like cracks seemed to come from every direction.

Gary pointed and Sue nodded, and without saying anything they were off again, trying a new direction to find the rams. Gary was almost running, carrying his gun uselessly at his side. Sue spread out and had hers at the ready, so when the Huns did come up, from near a low clump of juniper, she was firing before Gary knew they were there.

Gary turned when he heard the shot and watched her swing after the covey, and he saw a bird fold with her second shot. Without lifting his gun, he watched the covey belly down into the bottom, then lift back up and scrape over the ridgetop and disappear. He smiled watching their set-winged glides, and knew that loneliness only came here to let him know he wasn't simply a visitor.

He crossed through the dry grass and rocky soil to where Sue was picking up her bird. "I was too fast with the first one," she said. "It always seems like you'll never have enough time."

Gary nodded and smiled, and she held the little bird on its back in her hand. Then she looked at Gary and her smile turned into a laugh. "I saw your lightning reaction." She held her gun down, barrels pointed at the ground, and let her mouth drop open to a stupefied grin. "That's exactly how you looked." She shook her head and laughed again, reaching around him with the arm that held the bird.

When she let go, another of the jarring cracks drifted around them. Gary said it was cold enough that they could wait to gut the bird, and he started off to where he thought the rams might be.

Sue caught up with him in a second and touched his arm. "Take it easy," she said.

"Come on, Sue. We've got to see them."

"We've both seen them before, Gary. We will again. Hearing them's enough right now."

She held the bird out for him to see, and he remembered they were her favorite thing. It was funny how Huns went. They could run across them every day some weeks and then not see them again for a month.

Gary reached inside his coat and into his shirt pocket and pulled out one of the wishbones from his dinner. He held one end of the tiny bone. "I've been thinking we should move to Seattle, Sue. I could work with George."

Sue rolled her eyes and took the other end of the wishbone between her fingers. She smiled as if she were being forced to amuse him, but she knew the wishbone game was something his parents had always played with their children during what Gary always described as the lean years. "You'll find work, Gary. We're not going anyplace." She pinched tight on her half of the bone and said, "For staying in Montana forever."

They pulled away from each other, and the bone, so tiny it was already brittle, snapped. Sue held the longer piece. She gloated over her victory, and Gary dug out the second wishbone. "Two out of three," he said, knowing he didn't have a third.

She waved him away and said it didn't count if they always wished for things they'd get anyway, and what difference would it make who won if they were always wishing for the same things? She started away from him before he could say another word.

Gary watched her charge up the hill the partridge had disappeared behind, gun at the ready. Then he pulled the wishbone apart by himself. He threw away the short end and chased after her, waving the long piece. "I won," he shouted into the wind.

She turned at the ridgetop. "So we'll both stay in Montana," she shouted. "But I'll still shoot more Huns," she added, making the face imitating Gary watching the partridge fly away. She laughed then and dropped out of sight down the opposite side of the ridge, and Gary ran even faster to catch up.

King of the
Mountain

SEAN AND I DROVE out in his Range Rover to meet my old man. He'd never seemed that old to me, just my dad, but that's what Sean called his. We talked the whole way, nearly five hours, mostly wild drinking stories and tales of different girls we'd smooth-talked into nakedness and more. I had to stretch the truth for most of the drinking stories. I'd been legal age for a month but hadn't liked the idea of drinking for a long time before that. The other stories I pulled from thin air, using letters I'd read in *Penthouse* as a guide. But Sean, my roommate for my first two months of college, was from back East and seemed to have done everything.

He was excited about going hunting, but he didn't ask about it, like I'd kind of expected. He'd been deer hunting in Pennsylvania, and he talked a lot about that. He talked so much about drives and tree stands and buckshot and slugs and four-teen-point bucks that I began to wonder if Pennsylvania was on the same planet as Montana. A couple of times I tried to say that deer hunting was probably different out here, but then he'd start telling about a night at prom, about snaking some hot, innocent sophomore out of her long, formal dress, and I'd stop to listen.

I told him when to leave the highway and then when to leave the pavement, and he drove pretty fast over the washboard. The beer he held between his legs foamed up and stained his jeans. He made a dirty joke about it. I'd just taken a drink myself, and it came out my nose when I laughed. That only made it funnier, and I looked again at my watch and figured we wouldn't have time to hunt tonight anyway. So when Sean reached into the cooler for another beer, I did too. Drinking seemed fun with him. He barreled through a section of road the alder had grown tight around, and the branches screeched along the sides. "Montana pinstriping!" he yelled, and we toasted to that.

He was still going pretty fast when we got close to where Dad said we'd camp, and I told him to slow down. He did a little, but when I said, "That's us. That's the tent," he had to put on the brakes. We slid to a stop and our own dust cloaked us, the same way he said that girl's dress had billowed over her head. I wondered what my dad would think about that.

Dad slipped through the tent door about the same time the dust floated over us. He was smiling and shaking his head, and I smiled back. He was by himself and his hands were empty, and I felt bad that we'd been the ones to start the drinking.

When we got out of the truck, Sean still holding his beer, Dad chuckled and said, "I see." He stepped forward and shook my hand and asked how I was doing. I introduced him to Sean, and he said, "Ah, the famous Sean. Heard a lot about you already. Ready to get after some of these big bucks?"

"Damn right," Sean said, laughing, as sure of himself as I'd guessed he'd be. He was the first guy I'd ever tried to bring hunting.

I stepped into the tent, and Dad already had a fire going in the stove. That felt good. There was only one cot set up, and I asked where Ray, Dad's partner, was. "Working," Dad said. "Couldn't get away."

"I didn't expect you to have everything ready. I've been telling Sean how much work we'd have to do."

"I got out early. I was wondering if you guys were ever going to show." He pointed at Sean's beer. "Ready for a happy hour?" he asked. "Or am I already too late?"

I looked at my dad, but Sean said, "Always ready," and I laughed a little. Dad fished around in a grocery bag and lifted out a bottle of bourbon, one of the big, half-gallon bottles.

Sean said, "Whatchya got there?"

Dad raised his eyebrows and said, "Can I mix you a little toddy?" That's what he calls whiskey mixed with anything.

Sean said, "Sure," and Dad glanced at me. I shook my head without looking at him. "I don't like whiskey much," I said. "I might have a beer." I walked out to Sean's truck for the cooler. It was already chilly outside, a little breeze rattling through the dead cottonwood leaves. The sun was below the rim of mountains, and it was too late to go hunting. I carried the cooler back through the flap of the tent door.

Dad fixed dinner, three steaks that must've been most of a cow once, and he started telling stories while he and Sean pounded down the toddies. It seemed like they were having the time of their lives, and I tried keeping up for a while. But my ears began to buzz, and when Dad mixed another round I didn't open another beer. I don't like it to get even that far, but some of Dad's stories were awful funny, and this was about the only way they ever got out. I laughed until my sides ached when he told the one about the dog he'd trained to run alligators. It was his test, and when Sean just kept nodding like anything was possible, it was too much for me.

I rolled out my bag finally and said I was done. They laughed at me and called me names, but I turned my back to them and pulled the bag over my head. For a little while I was tense, wondering if they'd pinch the neck of the bag shut and haul me off somewhere, but then I heard Sean puking out alongside the tent, followed by my dad's thunderous horselaugh, so different from his shy smile when he first met us at the door of the tent. He bellowed, "Thought you were man enough to piss in the long grass, eh?" Sean groaned something, and I heard Dad pick him up and get him to bed, laughing and joking the whole time. Like he was the greatest guy in the world. I scrunched deeper into my bag.

I was up first in the morning, but Dad wasn't far behind. We went out and pissed, and it steamed into the air. "Your friend looks a little green around the gills this morning," he said.

I smiled, though it didn't seem funny. He kept looking at me, and I said, "He sure does." Once he starts my dad always kills off any camp newcomer. I'd hoped he'd give Sean a break, since he was a friend of mine. Maybe I'd even thought Sean might've stood a chance against him.

He said, "Think we should give the draws a try?"

"Whatever," I said.

"Wake up Sleeping Beauty then and we'll get a hunt in before lunch."

But there was no getting Sean out. He looked at me, his eyes bleeding into road maps, and I remembered how I'd planned on him and me hunting on our own if Dad got bad. He mumbled that he'd hit it hard in the evening, and I had to leave him there.

Dad and I went straight out from camp, each taking a side of a draw and paralleling each other, keeping our eyes open for anything we might push out. We each had an either-sex tag and a second antlerless tag. Once I saw a doe and two fawns slipping away in front of him, but I could see the wrinkle of ground that blocked them from his sight. I almost shouted over to him but stayed quiet instead and watched them get away.

When we hit the bottom, thick with willow and rose, we met up and side-hilled, wondering if a whitetail might not break out of the heavy stuff. But nothing did, and when the next draw unfolded, we started up it. This time Dad took the mostly open south face, slow walking between the towering ponderosas. I had tougher going through the firs and scrub, but Dad was careful to match my speed.

We could've used a third guy at the top, closing off the escape route, and I felt kind of embarrassed for Sean. And I wished he could've been waiting up there, watching my dad gliding up the steep parts, quiet and alert and careful, only caring about the hunting.

I was wondering what Sean's old man was like when Dad shot. The sudden, quick slap of his rifle made me jump. My heart raced, and I looked over just in time to see a string of does boiling over the rim on his side of the draw. He was hot-footing forward, and out in front of him I saw a doe down, not moving at all. "She's down," I yelled, and I started down to the bottom before climbing and meeting my dad over the deer.

By the time I got there, he already had the guts out, all shiny against the dust-dry, flinty dirt. But the air took the shine off them, and when he flipped the deer, the dust clung to the pile. He's the quickest, cleanest gutter I've ever seen. He smiled at me and asked if I'd seen them.

"It was too thick. I couldn't see anything. Did I kick them out?"

"Pretty as a picture."

We'd been out under two hours, and our breath still made clouds. He cut out the heart, careful to leave the sac around it so it wasn't all bloody, and he dropped it into the game pouch of his vest. He doesn't like anything the way he likes heart. Then he cracked the pelvis with his knife and flopped a leg at my head, so I had to catch it or get smacked, an old trick of his. He grinned. "Ready?"

"I guess," I said, and we started the short, hard drag to the crest.

We took a blow there, sweating hard, but because of the way we'd been looping around, we really weren't that far from camp. As we were dragging on the level, he said, "That Sean seems like an OK guy."

I said yeah he was or something like that, but I wondered what he really thought. He'd gone down like a ton of bricks last night, hardly a challenge for my dad. And before that, right when I pulled the sleeping bag over my head, Sean had started into one of his girl stories. He was drunk and a little hard to understand by then, but I'd cringed in my bag. You don't say stuff like that to anybody's dad.

"Real lady-killer," Dad said.

I shrugged and didn't say anything. I thought getting the deer so clean and easy might hop him over the morning part when he'd get mean. But now I knew he'd decided what he was going to pick on. "How about you?" he asked. "You out there chasing after it too?"

"Hell no!" I blurted, laughing a little nervously.

My dad laughed too, an odd, quiet chuckle, one I pretended I didn't recognize. "Well, old Sean sounds like the real McCoy," he said.

I said, "He talks a lot," though his stories had sounded believable enough when there'd just been the two of us.

"Most do," Dad said.

We left the deer at the road and walked back to the tent. My dad started putting the sneak on as we got close and I did the same, not knowing why. He peeked in the flap and slipped in quietly.

It was hot in the tent with the sun beating on the canvas, and Dad reached into the game pouch on the back of his vest. He pulled out a big chunk of the deer hide. He straightened it around, and I realized it was the doe's business end, the teats and all the rest.

He bent down and I whispered, "Dad!" but he went ahead anyway, draping that musty old thing right over Sean's face.

Sean sputtered a little and moved around, then sat up suddenly, pawing at his face. The green side of the hide was clammy and it stuck to Sean's hand. "Well, get after it boy!" Dad shouted. I turned and walked out of the tent. He didn't even sound like he was kidding.

I heard Sean say, "What the hell's this?"

"You gotta ask? A master like yourself?" He sounded mad, but after a moment of silence he bellowed, "Roll on out, boy. Chet and I already got one down and cleaned."

I climbed into our truck and just before I turned the key I heard him yell, "I plow deep while sluggards sleep!" his standard wake-up shout since I could remember.

When I got back with the deer, Dad and I hung it from the game pole. We were just tying it off when Sean came out. "It's a doe," he said, sounding scornful.

"Those are the only kind that have those parts," my dad said in the voice I'd learned to be careful around.

Maybe Sean could tell that much. He said, "It's a big one," and my dad said, "Damn right." A minute later he said, "You should've seen Chet push 'em out to me. Like clockwork," and I thought maybe we'd passed the worst of it.

We ate a huge breakfast, my dad cooking like always, though I could tell he was running out of steam, the night chasing hard after him. He always has that early burst, then passes out and isn't worth a damn the rest of the day unless he starts drinking again.

When the food was heavy in our stomachs, he pushed some stuff from his cot and spread out. "A little shut-eye," he said, "and we'll knock the stuffing out of them again this afternoon."

Sean had only pushed his breakfast around his plate, and he was back in his sleeping bag in a heartbeat, giving me a weak, little smile as I poured myself another cup of coffee.

I looked at them, my dad fully dressed on top of his sleeping bag, his mouth already open, his breathing getting louder, and I felt like shouting, "*I plow deep while sluggards sleep!*" but Dad wouldn't take it. Not in the morning.

It seemed too hot in the tent, and I took my coffee outside. Clouds were closing in, already leaving only straggly scraps of blue. I looked around our little camp at the edge of the trees, looking so much like our camps when I was a kid, and the coffee in my stomach went all acidy. I pitched what was left in my cup, swinging it wide and listening to the crunch of the downed leaves it hit. I picked my rifle up from the picnic table and started off in the opposite direction from the one I'd taken before with Dad.

For a long time there was nothing. I wasn't really hunting, more just putting distance between myself and the tent. But I'd drank too much too, and after a while I had to slow down. I started to hunt then, watching everything more carefully.

When I saw the set of ears just above the tangle of juniper, I sat down. Through the scope I could see that the deer was facing the other way, its ears switching this way and that, like it knew something was up but couldn't tell just what. Even the breeze was in my favor. It wasn't seventy yards away, and I knew I could take it anytime. But I settled into a comfortable spot and kept watching through the scope.

Every once in a while it would turn and look over its shoulder, but I was sitting still and it never made me out. The safety had been off since I first sat down, and I moved the cross hairs along her neck and head, imagining what each placement would do. Though I looked up and down the draw, it seemed she was all alone.

I kept her in the scope, but I started thinking about my dad; about Mom cutting his drinking off at home, until the hunt camp became something I never remembered it being. Though I was looking at the doe the whole time, I don't really remember seeing her get up. But there she was, standing, looking right up the hill at me. I don't know what tipped her off, a little curl of wind maybe. I lined up quick under her chin and pulled the trigger without a thought.

The recoil shocked the scope away from my eye and when I got it back all I could see was a little commotion in the juniper, flashes of writhing brown between the branches. I jacked in a new round and thumbed the rifle to safe. Then I walked down to the bush, and the deer wasn't moving at all anymore. I gutted her out, much more slowly and more carefully than Dad would've, but with the same result. It would've been impossible to tell different people had done the cleaning.

The drag wasn't nearly as easy by myself, and when I'd left the tent I hadn't been thinking well enough to work in loops, like my dad and I had. I had to drag her all the way back, with no road to help me, and the sweat dripped off my nose.

When I finally had her back, there was no sign of life from the tent. I went to the jug and drank water till I thought I'd burst. Then I carried the jug to the deer and washed her out. I was exhausted, and I watched the water run over her insides and out onto the ground, where it soaked in almost before it muddied the dirt. I wished I had the guts to dump Dad's big bottle that same way, so when he started in on it again tonight and found it empty I could say I'd cleaned my deer with it, and there wouldn't be anything for him to do but give me that clean, shy, sober smile of his.

I could've waited for either of them to get up, and my dad owed me a hand with it, but I hoisted that deer onto the rack by myself, so when he got up it'd be hanging there looking at him, all dead and finished. Then I went inside the tent and sat down in Dad's lawn chair, feeling tired. I ate an apple and tried not to look at them sleeping.

In a while I checked my watch. It was nearly three; time to be going again. I smiled a little and tossed the apple core onto Sean in his bag, but he didn't move. I glanced over at my dad, remembering how I'd planned on hunting with just Sean. I nudged Sean with my toe, but he still didn't move. Though I couldn't think of much I'd rather do less right then, I started to knock around some, on purpose, but neither one of them even fluttered an eyelid.

I kept staring at my dad. He'd really done a number on Sean. Finally I walked up to Dad's cot. I bent close to look at him. His breath was terrible. I whispered, "I plow deep while sluggards sleep." I wondered, if I ever had kids, if I'd be able to roust them out of bed with that friendly chant. I'd always looked forward to hearing it when I was little.

Suddenly I grabbed my dad by the armholes of his hunting vest and I shook him as hard as I could and I yelled, "*I* plow deep! *I* do! You don't do shit!" That's not at all what I meant to say, or even do, but I stood there shaking him until he sat up and pushed me away.

He'd been out hard and hadn't heard a word. He looked at me and blinked, his hair pointing in all the wrong directions. "What's the matter?" he said, sounding shy and confused.

I looked at him a moment more, then said, "Nothing. I got another doe. It's time to get going if we're going to get anything tonight." He kept looking at me, and I walked out of the tent, saying, "It's time to get going."

They both poked out of the tent at the same time and walked gingerly to my deer and checked her out. Dad looked pretty rough, but he managed to say, "Nice shot," and I felt bad about having shaken him so hard.

Sean asked, "How far?" He was fingering the hole in the back of her neck. I said, "It was close."

My dad dug in his pocket then, finding his truck keys, and said, "Let's try the mountain."

I said, "All right, but it's getting late."

"Plenty of time," he said, and he turned back for the tent.

I shouted after him, "Brush your teeth." He turned and gave that little smile. I realized that was always the last thing he used say to me at night, after the kiss and the swat on the rear. I said, "Your breath is terrible."

"'Xactlies," he said, slipping into the tent.

"'Xactlies?" Sean asked.

"When your mouth tastes 'xactly like your asshole."

Sean laughed and said he had a case of them himself. He dug his toothbrush out of his pack, which he'd never even taken out of his truck last night.

When Dad came out I was telling Sean about where we were going and what it would be like. I'd told him things about the mountain before, at school. He seemed interested to know things now. He said he was sorry he'd slept through two deer already, but then he chuckled and said he still doubted he could walk far tonight. "Your old man can really put it away," he said.

"Yeah," I said, looking at the way the clouds raced along. "Isn't it great?"

"Yeah. If my old man ever caught me puking drunk I'd be dead meat."

Dad came out then and settled his rifle into the gun rack and fired up the truck, cradling a red can of Coke between his legs. I scrunched over next to him, and Sean rode shotgun, holding his rifle between his knees. We were nearly to the mountain when Dad hit some old ruts wrong and some of his Coke went flying, and I was able to smell what was in the can. When we piled out of the truck, Dad was getting perky again.

We were in the bottom of the gap in the mountain, which was really just a big hill, the biggest one around. We stood there a minute, working the stiffness out of our legs, and Dad didn't even try to hide it when he took a regular-size bottle out of his toolbox and added some to his Coke. I wondered if there was any Coke in there at all. I wondered if he'd take his gun out. I wondered if he'd gone that far.

Usually Dad makes the plans, but when he started to say something to Sean about toddies, I said, "You head straight off here, Sean, and round this edge. That puts you into a pretty nice meadow. It's not far, and if you don't feel like walking, it's a pretty good place to sit and wait."

Dad looked at me a second. The clouds had spread out again, enough to let some sun through, and I pointed to the ridge that faced the west. "I'll go up there and work back around. They might be up there catching the last of the sun. If I can I'll try to spook them back through the meadow to you, Sean." I'd taken my rifle from the rack as I talked. I was talking too fast, and I wondered if Sean had been able to understand me. "Or you can come with me if you want," I added.

Sean smiled, looking up the hill where I was going. "I think I'll sit in the meadow," he said.

Dad kept looking at me, and I shouldered my gun. "Aren't you going to tell me what to do?" he asked as soon as I started walking.

I wanted to keep going, but I stopped and turned around. "You're not going to hunt, are you?"

He just kept looking at me. He took a sip from his can.

"OK," I said. "You stay here. We'll be back at dark. It won't be long." I started walking away again. "Have yourself a toddy," I said, plenty loud for him to hear. I was sweating before I even started the climb.

I paused when the truck was a long way back and out of sight. I could see Sean about half a mile away, just about to the meadow, his orange vest a dot in all the brown and green below the line of sunlight. I kept going, turning up the ridge, the sun hardly feeling hot enough to warm me but nice to have all the same. It was a long time before I saw the string of deer single-filing along the high, open face of the hill, easy to pick out in the sun.

They were out of range and they were heading back toward the truck, not toward the meadow. I scoped them for a second and saw that a big four-point was following up the string of does. First buck we'd seen.

I looked back to where Sean was sitting, but I couldn't see him now. There was no way to turn these deer to him. It'd be a long shot getting to them myself. I felt bad that I'd put him in the wrong place, though I'd really thought I'd given him the best chance. I smiled a little, thinking how he was probably asleep by now anyway.

I dropped back below the lip of hill I'd just crested, and I started to run back in the direction of the truck. I'd gained a lot of elevation, and though I hated to, I had to give most of it up to keep the little ridge between me and the deer. I was puffing like a mule by the time I reached the neck of trees I'd picked out as the place I'd go up and have some cover and still some chance of cutting them off.

I wanted to give myself a second to catch my breath, but I knew I didn't have time. I started up the hill, darting from ponderosa to ponderosa as much as I could. I tried to keep an eye out for the deer, but mostly I had to watch the ground so I could hop from rock to rock without breaking my neck.

When the deer started to cross the timber above me, not sixty yards away, I was already behind a tree, but I was panting so hard I could barely hold my scope on a single animal. They hadn't made me and they ambled along, each going through the same clear spot, and I tried to calm down and wait for the buck, but all of a sudden he was there, the last one through, and my gun was still bouncing all over the place. It seemed there was nothing in the scope but antlers, huge antlers that didn't make anything any easier. I only had a second, and I tried to time the bounce of the cross hairs and aim into his boiler room at the same time. I let one fly.

This time, by the time I had the scope back to my eye, there was nothing to see. I lowered the rifle and looked around and saw the rears of a few deer disappear. They'd jumped the trail and started straight up the hill, same as muleys always do, going up a little ways and then turning around to see if anything's following.

I watched the dark patch of timber the buck had been about to enter, and I couldn't see a thing in there. Then I thought I heard something solid. Like a big thing falling all at once. I smiled, already not sure if I'd really heard it, or if it had really sounded like what I hoped it was. I started creeping forward, having to stop when I remembered I hadn't jacked in a second shell yet.

I held my gun at the ready, thumb all set to flip off the safety, and I edged into the dark patch. I took a few more steps, my heart going hard, but not from the uphill anymore. Then I saw him, down in the duff, some of it scraped up by his hooves. Where it was torn it was darker than the rest. His antlers had hung up in the same mess of dirt and rock and long, old needles, so that while he was lying on his side, his legs pointing up the hill, his head was twisted around, resting back on his rack, looking straight up into the last of the sunlight. A steady wisp of steam drifted out of his open mouth, then stopped.

I was trembling a little by the time I got to him. I'd shot bucks before, but nothing like this one at all. Usually we took whatever came first, mostly does or forkies. I smiled and reached down to touch him. Dad wouldn't believe it even when he saw it. He'd had his best mounted when I was a kid. I'd spent years staring and staring at it over the TV. This one looked like its big brother. He wouldn't believe his eyes.

Since I was on the side hill, I dragged him down out of the thicket before I started to gut him. I had an idea it would be nice to be in the sun, but by the time I had him turned head uphill out in the open, the sun was past me, only just touching the top of the mountain over my head. I started the knife into him, hoping Dad would still be sober enough to tell stories about this one someday.

I planned how I would tell it to him; how I would make him laugh when I told how I'd run like a madman down the ridge, then turned up the mountain, sweat pouring in buckets off my face, and how the gun had almost danced out of my hands I was so out of breath, and how that heavy, solid whump had sounded so final in the dark patch where I couldn't see, where I was afraid to tell myself it was true.

I dumped the guts, keeping the heart in its own sac the way he'd taught me, and I listened to how the story would sound in some perfect hunt camp of the future, me sitting quiet while he made up all the details he'd missed by staying at the truck. It would seem like I knew everything, and parts of it he'd make funny enough to die for, but in the end, no matter what else got added, I would always make that perfect, impossible shot.

I was smiling wide enough to break, and I was trembling more over how his stories would sound than I had over the deer. Then the gigantic rip of sound so close made me leap, and I cut myself with my gutting knife, and even as my head was replaying the sound, separating the blast from the tearing whistle of the bullet, I felt the sting of water in the corners of my eyes, squeezed out by the force of the shot and the skipped beat of my own heart. I shouted, "I'm right here!" and I dove behind my deer before I realized that was probably the worst place to be. I glanced up and saw a ponderosa at the edge of the dark patch and I crawled for it, shouting, "I'm right here! I'm right here!"

I circled the tree and finally looked around, and there on the knob of hill behind me was my dad. He was kneeling up so he could see, and he was holding his rifle loose at his side, still pointing at me. He was staring at me, and even though he was a good fifty yards away I knew I'd never seen anything like that fear or shock on his face. I shouted, "I'm right here!" again, just because I couldn't make anything else come out of my mouth.

"Damn, you scared me," he said, in a big, relieved rush of breath.

"I scared you?" I shouted.

"They're all over the hill above you," he said, starting to wipe that look off his face. "Get behind that tree and I'll take another shot. I missed."

He was already bringing his rifle up again, and I hunkered behind the wide, friendly trunk of that pine. I could count the number of times he'd missed on one hand. The same crashing tear sounded out, but it wasn't as big this time, knowing it was coming. I realized the first shot hadn't really been that close.

"Damn it!" Dad shouted, laughing a little. "You scared me so bad I'm shaking like a leaf. Knock one of those things down for me, would you?"

I poked my head around the tree to look at him, and he was standing up, in full view of the deer. I glanced up the hill, and the deer were well on their way to being long gone. I couldn't have knocked one down with a rocket.

"Don't shoot," I said, but he was already shouldering his rifle, coming down to me.

He was chuckling some, getting ready to laugh everything off. I brushed the startled edge of tears out of the corners of my eyes. "You made me cut myself," I said.

His chuckling was getting ahold of him and he started singing, "I'm right here, I'm right here," in some sort of weird falsetto.

Then I could hear all the stories years from now—how I'd bleated, "I'm right here," over and over again and dug my face into the ground and crawled around hugging trees, and how I'd let the deer get away because I'd scared him so bad by shouting like that. I heard every one of his stories about it, and I realized I was still holding the heart I'd cut out for him.

When he reached me he whistled and said, "My God, you shot the king of the mountain," and I said, "Don't say a word about it. Not one word. Not ever."

He looked at me, and I could tell he knew what I meant and he knew how he'd done everything wrong, but I could also see he had enough in him to feel invincible and that he thought he could joke me around this one too. Who knows, maybe he could even see ahead to how he'd be in the morning. I'd never thought he did that, but the way he looked at me, all cocky with that you'll-grow-up look, I guessed maybe he saw that if the joking and the stories wouldn't work tonight, he could get ugly tomorrow and make me change my mind.

When he bent down to take a leg I stepped in his way. I said, "Don't even touch it."

When he started to look up, I thrust the heart at him. It just touched his chest, leaving a little smear of blood on his orange. "Take this," I said. "I saved it for you."

I wanted to heave it at him. I wanted it to hit him so hard it'd knock his smug, drunk assurance clean out of him. But I handed it to him and he just shrugged. "You want to drag it out, be my guest," he said. "But I owe you one from this morning, and I'd give you a hand."

"Damn right you owe me one," I said, not even knowing myself exactly what I meant, and I threw myself into dragging the deer down the mountain away from him. I shouted over to the meadow, where I still couldn't see a trace of Sean, "Hey, Sean. Come and check this one out." There was no answer for a moment, then a faint, "What?" drifted up out of the bottom.

Dad didn't say anything and I didn't look back that way.

"Come on up here and give me a hand with this thing," I shouted. "I got the king of the whole damn mountain."